Top Notes

T0360047

Stephen Daldry's
Billy Elliot
Study notes for Common Module:
Texts and Human Experiences
2019–2023 HSC

Bruce Pattinson
& Julia Walters

A
FIVE SENSES
PUBLICATION

Five Senses Education Pty Ltd
2/195 Prospect Highway
Seven Hills 2147
New South Wales
Australia

Pattinson, Bruce & Walters, Julia
Top Notes – Billy Elliot
ISBN 978-1-76032-214-4

CONTENTS

TOP NOTES SERIES

This series has been created to assist HSC students of English in their understanding of set texts. Top Notes are easy to read, providing analysis of issues and discussion of important ideas contained in the texts.

Particular care has been taken to ensure that students are able to examine each text in the context of the module it has been allocated to.

Each text generally includes:

- Notes on the specific module
- Plot summary
- Character analysis
- Setting
- Thematic concerns
- Language studies
- Essay questions and a modelled response
- Other textual material
- Study practice questions
- Useful quotes

We have covered the areas we feel are important for students in their study of *Texts and Human Experiences* for their Common Module. I am sure you will find these Top Notes useful in your studies of English.

Bruce Pattinson
Series Editor

COMMON MODULE: TEXTS AND HUMAN EXPERIENCES

"It is quite possible—overwhelmingly probable, one might guess—that we will always learn more about human life and personality from novels than from scientific psychology"

NOAM CHOMSKY

What is the Common Module?

The Common Module set for the 2019–23 HSC is *Texts and Human Experiences*. It is compulsory to study this topic as prescribed by NESA and it is common to all three English courses. Remember: you will be learning how texts reveal individual and collective human experiences. There are no right or wrong answers in this module – it is about how you see and interpret material and engage with it.

In the Common Module you will be analysing one prescribed text and a range of short texts that are related to the idea of human experiences. You will analyse texts not only to investigate the ideas they present about this area but also how they convey these ideas. This means you will be looking closely at the techniques a composer uses to represent his / her messages and shape meaning. You will also be looking at relationships between texts in regard to the experiences you explore. Overall, you will become an expert on texts and the human experience — that is, the different notions people have about human experience and the various ways composers manipulate techniques to communicate their ideas about it.

Specifically you will look at one set text from the following list.

- Doerr, Anthony, *All the Light We Cannot See*
- Lohrey, Amanda, *Vertigo*
- Orwell, George, *Nineteen Eighty-Four*
- Parrett, Favel, *Past the Shallows*
- Dobson, Rosemary 'Young Girl at a Window', 'Over the Hill', 'Summer's End', 'The Conversation', 'Cock Crow', 'Amy Caroline', 'Canberra Morning'
- Slessor, Kenneth 'Wild Grapes', 'Gulliver', 'Out of Time', 'Vesper-Song of the Reverend Samuel Marsden', 'William Street', 'Beach Burial'
- Harrison, Jane, *Rainbow's End*
- Miller, Arthur, *The Crucible*
- Shakespeare, William, *The Merchant of Venice*
- Winton, Tim, *The Boy Behind the Curtain* Chapters: 'Havoc: A Life in Accidents', 'Betsy', 'Twice on Sundays', 'The Wait and the Flow', 'In the Shadow of the Hospital', 'The Demon Shark', 'Barefoot in the Temple of Art'
- Yousafzai, Malala & Lamb, Christina, *I am Malala*
- Daldry, Stephen, *Billy Elliot*
- O'Mahoney, Ivan, *Go Back to Where You Came From –* Series 1, Episodes 1, 2 and 3 and *The Response*
- Walker, Lucy, *Waste Land*

NESA has mandated that students must study a related text as part of the common module, and that this should be part of their in-school assessment. However there is NO LONGER a requirement to write about a related text in the HSC examination itself.

WHAT DOES NESA REQUIRE FOR THE COMMON MODULE?

The NESA documentation of the Common Module: Texts and Human Experiences states that students:

- deepen their understanding of how texts represent individual and collective human experiences;

- examine how texts represent human qualities and emotions associated with, or arising from, these experiences;

- appreciate, explore, interpret, analyse and evaluate the ways language is used to shape these representations in a range of texts in a variety of forms, modes and media;

- explore how texts may give insight into the anomalies, paradoxes and inconsistencies in human behaviour and motivations, inviting the responder to see the world differently, to challenge assumptions, ignite new ideas or reflect personally;

- may also consider the role of storytelling throughout time to express and reflect particular lives and cultures;

- by responding to a range of texts, further develop skills and confidence using various literary devices, language concepts, modes and media to formulate a considered response to texts;

- study one prescribed text and a range of short texts that provide rich opportunities to further explore representations of human experiences illuminated in texts;

- make increasingly informed judgements about how aspects of these texts, for example, context, purpose, structure, stylistic and grammatical features, and form shape meaning;

- select one related text and draw from personal experience to make connections between themselves, the world of the text and their wider world;

- by responding and composing throughout the module, further develop a repertoire of skills in comprehending, interpreting and analysing complex texts;

- examine how different modes and media use visual, verbal and/or digital language elements;

- communicate ideas using figurative language to express universal themes and evaluative language to make informed judgements about texts;

- further develop skills in using metalanguage, correct grammar and syntax to analyse language and express a personal perspective about a text

If this is what is required by NESA, we need to examine the concept of human experience carefully so we can adequately respond in these ways. I would recommend that you read the complete document which is on the NESA web site and can be downloaded in Word or Adobe. Understanding this document is an important step in handling the textual material within the guidelines required — remember you are reading for a purpose and should make notes and highlight ideas as you read so that you can develop these ideas later.

UNDERSTANDING THE COMMON MODULE

What are Human Experiences?

The concept of Human Experiences is at the heart of the Common Module.

Human Experiences are experiences of individuals or a group of people (eg a family, society, or nation) in life. There are a very wide range of human experiences which include but go beyond this list:

- feelings or reactions (momentary or long term): love, hate, anger, joy, fear, disgust
- key milestones or stages: birth, childhood, adulthood, marriage, divorce, death
- culture, belonging and identity
- conformity and rebellion
- innocence and guilt, justice
- freedom and repression
- education, vocation, work, sport, leisure
- attraction to a person, idea, group or cause
- opposition to an idea, cause, political system
- religious faith or belief
- extreme events such as an earthquake, avalanche, tsuanami
- regular events such as walking, eating, singing, dancing, discussing ideas.

The word *experience* seems innately connected to the human condition and it is something we have each day whether a mundane experience that is repetitive, or something new and dramatic which offers challenges and rewards. Experiences can vary greatly in their impact on individuals, groups and countries. One example might be a war that is a negative experience for a whole population while we may experience the wonder of medicine with a new vaccine for a deadly disease that saves millions of people. We need to note that the module asks for 'experiences' ...we are a combination of different experiences and each has a varying impact. One person's problem is another's challenge depending on perspective, skill set, previous experience and ability.

Experiences are widespread and often shared: this is why people tell their stories and these shared experiences form part of our cultural heritage. These experiences often inform, warn and teach across entire cultural groups and many stories are shared across cultures.

DEFINING HUMAN EXPERIENCES

Now let's attempt to define what human experiences are and shape them into a more coherent and easily understood framework so we can begin our investigation at a basic level of understanding before moving into more complex analysis and looking at how the texts illuminate our understanding of the term.

Dictionary.com defines the term **experience** as:

noun

1. a particular instance of personally encountering or undergoing something:

2. the process or fact of personally observing, encountering, or undergoing something:

3. the observing, encountering, or undergoing of things generally as they occur in the course of time:
   to learn from experience; the range of human experience.

4. knowledge or practical wisdom gained from what one has observed, encountered, or undergone, e.g. *a man of experience.*

5. *Philosophy.* the totality of the cognitions given by perception; all that is perceived, understood, and remembered.

verb

(used with object), **experienced, experiencing.**

6. to have experience of; meet with; undergo; feel, e.g. *to experience nausea.*

7. to learn by experience.

idiom

8. **experience religion**, to undergo a spiritual conversion by which one gains or regains faith in God.

Obviously there are a number of definitions according to context, but all are applicable to our study in some shape or form, as the range of human experience is so vast. The search for 'new experience' has driven much of the development of people, groups, cultures and nations over past millennia. New experiences are always met with excitement and often trepidation as to what change they might bring.

Think historically about how people have reacted to change. It can cause great upheavals in society, with violent reactions while other changes brought through various experiences are welcomed and may change how people live and comprehend the world. Experiences affect us emotionally in many cases rather than logically and when we respond emotionally, behaviours become unpredictable. This causes the paradoxes, anomalies and inconsistencies mentioned in the rubric. If we were logical beings the world would be an easier place, but probably more boring.

These definitions all point to the fact that memory is the key to experience. The experience is stored in memory and drawn upon when the circumstances are repeated or closely mimicked so we can deal with them — hopefully better than on the initial experience.

Experiences can come in many ways and the synonyms listed below for experience help us to understand the concept even further. They assist in defining how an experience can arise:

Synonyms

actions

background

contacts

involvement

know-how

maturity

participation

patience

practice

reality

sense

skill

struggle

training

understanding

wisdom

acquaintances

actuality

caution

combat

doings

empiricism

evidence

existences

exposures

familiarity

intimacy

inwardness

judgment

observation

perspicacity

practicality

proofs

savoir-faire

seasonings

sophistication

strife

trials

worldliness

forebearance

http://www.thesaurus.com/browse/experience?s=t

These synonyms show partly the vast array of words that our language has created around this concept, and also shows how important it is in the human psyche. We, as humans, want to experience. Now we will look at some examples of experiences and examine how they can have an impact. It is also important to remember that experiences do not have to be positive. You might experience a huge problem, a bereavement, a car accident, an unwelcome relationship or something totally bizarre that rocks your world. There can be a more opaque side to any experience that may need to be addressed.

The whole aim of this Common Module is to examine the text closely but also relate it to the concept of human experiences and decide how examining it in this way enables us to better understand both the text and the concept of humanity.

It is important that you unpack what each text you study shows you about human experiences and what ideas / themes arise from those experiences. Formulate your own ideas about the text.

Read the NESA Stage 6 document called *English Stage 6: Annotations of selected texts prescribed for the Higher School Certificate 2019–23* (see *www.educationstandards.nsw.edu.au*) for the set text you are studying. This document offers insights into the way each particular text should be examined by outlining key ideas and areas for clarification.

Human experiences and ways of experiencing vary due to individual circumstance and these experiences can change many things about individual lives, communities and the world. When we examine the concept of human experience in relation to a text, we need to examine the assumptions or biases we bring to it as well as how experiencing the text itself may change us and how we view things. The text may challenge and confront how we view the human experience or we may have preconceived ideas that make it more difficult for this to happen.

Students can also think about their own 'personal experience to make connections between themselves, the world of the text and their wider world.' Examining and enjoying any text is an experience in itself but it is what we take away from the text and apply that is the crucial aspect. That is not to say that every text will be enjoyed or offer a human experience that is significant either positively or negatively. Some texts may not personally engage you and that is fine. This is especially so when you begin to look for other related material that links to *Texts and Human Experiences*. We recommend that you find examples of texts that link but also personally appeal to you so that you can relate empathetically with them.

Individual Human Experiences

The idea of personal experiences is a popular and pervasive concept, especially in the literature of many cultures. Recording personal experiences as a means of sharing wisdom or more mundane daily tasks is part of human nature and we record and relate these experiences frequently. Experiences are recorded and relayed in many ways. We tell oral stories in both anecdotal and formal ways, we write, draw, sing and photograph our way into history (or not). Look at the proliferation of social media in this current century as people record their daily, even hourly, experiences for all to see. We record the most trivial details of our lives for likes and followers while the real world passes us by. Human experiences affect us on a daily basis and some experiences influence our lives and the way we live them.

Individuals seek out experiences in a variety of ways. Some seek more and more extreme experiences to test themselves against the world. Others limit their experiences. A lot of people prefer the familiar and don't actively seek new experiences. Individuals, it must be remembered, also see experiences in different ways and the same experience may have a very different impact on individuals. The one thing we can be certain about is that experiences are part of humanity and even the most limited of us have them. Many of these experiences also come from interaction with others and as noted we also like to share these experiences.

Experiences are what define us in many ways and are what makes us human.

We are going to look at four specific ways that experiences can influence us as people over the next few pages. These are physical, psychological, emotional and intellectual experiences and many experiences are a combination of these.

Physical Experience

The concept of a physical experience is tied into the human experience and part of the collective experience as well. Individuals seek physical experiences to test themselves against nature and other individuals often as part of trials and rituals, for example being integrated into a community. In modern times individuals have sought to test themselves with extreme sports and explorations into the harshest conditions and even space. Physical experiences can also change the way we see the world and others because of the chemical changes these experiences have on our bodies and mind. Physical experiences are often challenges and part of the experience is overcoming adversity. These physical challenges are often celebrated, as in the case of sports, but can also offer challenges if the experience is a negative one such as an accident or disease. Physical experiences are also often quite public and thus have permeated our societies in both their execution and how they are perceived. These physical experiences, even if experienced vicariously, have become popular across cultures and celebrated. Think of examples for yourself but most competitive sports offer examples.

Bruce Lee extends the concept of the physical experience into all aspects of life and that's what we will look at next in our analysis of human experiences –

'If you always put limits on everything you do, physical or anything else, it will spread into your work and into your life. There are no limits. There are only plateaus, and you must not stay there, you must go beyond them.'

Psychological Experience

The idea of a psychological experience is tied into many of the abstract ideas that people experience and can lead to a discussion of what is normal psychology. From the earliest times humans have attempted to alter their psychology through a number of experiences. On a simple level this can be a drug that changes the person's or group's perspective on reality. Examples of this might be alcohol or marijuana but cultural groups also use various substances to share group experiences. This can be seen in Native American cultures with *peyote*. In more modern times prescription drugs that are mood altering have been used to minimise the symptoms of psychiatric illnesses such as depression, and these mood altering drugs are common and legal. Others attempt to alter their psychology by seeing specialists in this area while others act out their condition leading to social and criminal issues. When discussing the human experience, psychology is a key issue and will form a part of most studies of experience. When taken too far this search for a new psychological experience can be harmful eg. an addiction.

Carl Jung, the famous psychologist, comments on the problems of addiction for human experiences, stating clearly that excess can be an issue:

"Every form of addiction is bad, no matter whether the narcotic be alcohol, morphine or idealism."

Emotional Experience

According to the psychologist, Robert Plutchik, there are eight basic emotions:

- **Fear** — feeling afraid.
- **Anger** — feeling angry. A stronger word for anger is rage.
- **Sadness** — feeling sad. Other words are sorrow, grief (a stronger feeling, for example when someone has died) or **depression** (feeling sad for a long time without any external cause). Some people think depression is a different emotion.
- **Joy** — feeling happy. Other words are happiness, gladness.
- **Disgust** — feeling something is wrong or nasty
- **Trust** — a positive emotion; admiration is stronger; **acceptance** is weaker
- **Anticipation** — in the sense of looking forward positively to something which is going to happen. **Expectation** is more neutral; **dread** is more negative.

https://simple.wikipedia.org/wiki/List_of_emotions

Emotions are the strongest drivers of human experience and form lasting aspects of any experience. Think about breaking up with someone you love and the emotions that drive behaviours in this situation. People have all sorts of extreme behaviours under the influence of emotions and these experiences are often the ones recorded and those which influence us most. Think about the role emotions play in our lives and the range of emotions from the list above. Consider how much emotions affect our life experiences, how they influence our decisions which decide our experiences and on a higher level consider how they affect the decisions which may seriously impact our experiences, such as politicians going to war.

Intellectual Experience

The concept of an intellectual experience is linked to decisions and experiences we have based on analysis and logic rather than the emotional choices referred to in the previous section. These intellectual experiences have changed the way we live and how we have seen our world. These experiences have affected the way we as humans have altered our world to suit our needs and lead to all the great advances in human society and thus experiences. Changes in our ideas, beliefs etc. alter the way we interact with the world and often these intellectual changes come at great cost.

Think of the time in Europe when the Church dominated and stopped scientific advances by calling them heresy / witchcraft. Open societies are more open to new ideas and this is what has hastened the pace of intellectual experiences as dominant ideologies fall away. Intellectual advances may not have the excitement that the other types produce but perhaps they have a more lasting impact on people, societies and the world in general. Ideas are powerful experiences and people hold beliefs strongly.

Immanuel Kant stated that:

> "experience without theory is blind, but theory without experience is mere intellectual play."

Consider this statement in the light of what we have learnt about human experiences. Are they a combination of many factors or can we isolate experiences into simple forms?

What exactly is a human experience?

The titular question reminds us of the old brainteaser: "If a tree falls in a forest and no one is around to hear it, does it make a sound?"

There are two classic responses to this. The more Platonically-minded would say the tree always makes a sound when it falls in the forest. We don't have to be there to hear it; we can imagine the sound of a tree falling in the forest, based on memory of such an event or on the recording of such an event. We know that sound is just vibrating air, and it's safe to say that air always vibrates in response to a tree falling, or a bear growling, or a cicada singing, whether we are there to hear it or not.

The second answer is a more post-structuralist response: the sound doesn't occur on its own; it needs a human ear to be heard. Therefore, if there is no human in the forest to hear the tree fall, then there is no sound. This automatically implies that "experience" of anything requires the presence of a human being, which means there is no such thing as an experience that *isn't* human.

Animal rights activists – or anyone with a beloved pet – would almost certainly reject this notion because it prioritises humans and relegates all other species to a lower class of being: an attitude that most would agree has gotten the human race into an awful lot of environmental trouble over the last 200 years of industrialisation.

In his article (*What is an Experience?*), my learned colleague Paul Hartley describes experience in its most basic form, as "the perception of something else" and "ultimately information about what we have perceived." But does this make it particularly human? Dogs and cats perceive things. Insects perceive things. You could even say that plants perceive things, such as the direction from which the sun is shining. Perception is the most basic of life's survival tools for all manner of flora and fauna.

In her brief but cogent disquisition on the subject (*What is Human?*), another of my learned colleagues, Nadine Hare, asserts that to be human is a social construct. Hartley builds on that notion by suggesting that culture affects experience when we start to share it, because "the words, associations, and priorities we attach to the shared experience define how we understand the world we live in."

Hare rightly points out that this world is increasingly dominated by consumerism, which has distorted what it means to be human by excluding all of the attributes and qualities that "make people people." Calling us consumers reduces our experiences to mere transactions. It defines human experience within the narrow confines of the purchase funnel and has little interest in anything that isn't a purchase driver.

Perhaps the field of commerce is where the experiential rubber most emphatically meets the road. Unlike mere perception, commerce is a uniquely human experience. It has mediated, automated, and dominated the human agenda to the point where we are defined by what we buy and little else. Commerce has invaded the non-profit spheres of government, health, and education, imposing its own priorities and principles on these institutions in the expectation that they will behave more like businesses. And even though business still strives to appeal to the so-called masses, it prioritises the pursuit of individual wealth, and in so doing, not only inhibits the desire for shared experience but unravels the social fabric historically woven by the democratic tradition.

As if in response, that social fabric is being re-woven by our networks. As Hare asserts, "humans both produce technology and are produced through technology." Experience is shared more now than it ever has been because the experiential platform – i.e., that very human invention called the internet – is in place to facilitate it like never before, and on a global scale.

This sharing capability reintroduces all of those things that "make people people" back into the conversation – whether commercial or political. What "makes people people" is messy, unpredictable, emotional, and complex. Most of what makes us human has no place in the experiential confines of the purchase funnel, and defies any of our attempts to place it there.

The challenge for us as a species is to embrace this new capacity for sharing to keep the agendas of our hegemonic institutions – whether commercial or political – from defining what makes an experience human. A post-consumer business strategy might be one that, as Hare hopes, will "expand our view of people to include the complex and dynamic social, cultural, gendered, spiritual and racialised beings that they are." Maybe then will our shared human experience truly become, as Hartley asserts, the glue that holds us all together as human beings.

Will Novosedlik
MISC magazine

https://miscmagazine.com/what-is-a-human-experience/

This article appeared in the September 2014 edition of MISC magazine. Can you relate to what the article says about human experiences? Do human experiences depend on perception? Does the experience of anything require the presence of a human as experiencer (para 3)? Can the ideas of experience be extended to include perception by plants or animals? Hartley's idea is that "shared human experience" is "the glue that holds us all together as human beings". Is this an oversimplification?

The Impact of Human Experiences

Human experiences have impacts on many levels. On an individual level, we can have changes in our assumptions about the world and people around us; we can ingest new ideas and have these open new vistas of productivity and performance. We can also reflect and build on these experiences to ensure that they are even more meaningful to our lives. Behaviours towards others and the way we respond to the world can manifest themselves in new and different responses. An example might be that through adverse experiences we can build resilience so that the next negative experience isn't as traumatic and we accept it for what it is. Experiences also teach us new behaviours on a very physical level — if you burn yourself once on a flame you learn not to do it again (hopefully).

The impact of human experiences can also be shared in groups and societies. Firstly, let's examine some group dynamics that can be affected by human experiences. Groups share experiences and adapt and develop behaviours that impact on the group as a whole. Think about the notorious 'bonding' sessions sporting teams have that unite them in a common goal. Think about the behaviours of various gangs in our society. We see plenty of examples of this on American television where gangs based on ethnicity and social groupings form specific sets of behaviours that impact on how they interact with each other and the world. These groupings carry assumptions about how they see the world and respond to it. For example, they may have generally negative reactions to law enforcement and this is ingrained into their codes of behaviour. They are suspicious of the world and the people in it — dividing them up into threats, the law and victims. These behaviours are often reinforced by group experiences such as the initiation rituals which are integral to membership.

Often the impact of these behaviours is to perpetuate stereotypes that then categorise the individuals within these groups. The graphic I have included here shows a stereotypical gang member with the suspicious gaze, ubiquitous hoody and scruffy look. These stereotypes reject new ideas and maintain assumptions about the world, often to the detriment of their members. The experiences they have reinforce their own stereotypical way of viewing anything outside the safety of the group and the cycle continues. Of course, other groups have more positive impacts and see the world as a very different place and their experiences are designed to be positive interactions. Think about groups such as Rotary who are constructive in the community. Other groups have specialty interests such as Animal Welfare, Surf Lifesaving and charities.

Normal social interactions impact groups and individuals, but it takes a major event to alter the behaviours of whole societies, especially so in the modern world where societies are large in scale. Earlier in human history smaller experiences could alter the behaviour of societies as they were insignificant in size compared to modern ones. We often fail to remember that many of these ancient societies' behaviours were impacted by superstition, religions and cultural habituation. The modern society as we know it is only a recent phenomenon. Just a few hundred years ago with church rule people were forced to think in a specific

way and punished for not adhering to a theological culture. Think of the Spanish Inquisition, the imprisonment of Galileo and other such restrictions on freedom of thought; scientific breakthroughs were hidden or declared witchcraft. Even recently the world has seen societies kept repressed by failed ideologies. The brutality of such regimes has left deep scars on the social psyche of nations as they try to recover. This has had an impact on the human experiences of whole populations, and societies respond accordingly.

One example might be at the conclusion of the Communist regime in East Germany when the Berlin Wall was destroyed as a visual symbol of the new-found freedom of a whole population of people who had been repressed for decades by a brutal and ever-present regime. Many citizens who had grown up in this system, where you could 'disappear' without trial or real evidence, found the idea that you could express yourself incredible. Many of the

East Germans couldn't believe that this freedom was real and that the Stasi (the secret police) were gone.

Other experiences can affect societies in extreme ways. Think about wars and the impact they have on civilian populations.

Climatic events such as earthquakes change the way that people behave and respond to situations. Catastrophic flooding occurred in the US city of New Orleans in 2005. The US President's response to help was not immediate and the national administration was severely criticised for lack of effective action.

Societies also respond to perceived problems such as pollution. In 1989 the oil tanker Exxon Valdez ran aground in Prince William Sound, Alaska with disastrous results. The effects of this event are still being experienced thirty years later.

Societies can be divided, as we saw with the election of Donald Trump in the United States of America and the reaction of the Political Left.

The impact of human experiences on societies can be quite dramatic, as we have seen, while other experiences (such as an election) can go by without a murmur from societies, no matter who wins. As a last thought before we move on you should also consider the impact of the media on societies in the modern world, and how they influence individuals, societies and the development of ideas.

Problems With Human Behaviour

So far, we have discussed the impact of human experiences on behaviour. Now we can begin to develop some more complex judgements and understandings about the impact of those experiences on human behaviours. In simplistic terms it could be assessed as:

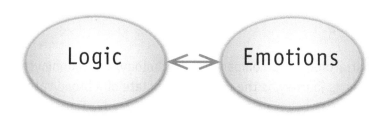

These two opposites on the continuum certainly shape the manner in which we see incidents and how they affect the experience. For instance, if someone you love has no interest in you, it creates a very different reaction to someone you don't care about having no interest in you. It is generally agreed that humans respond more strongly with emotion than they do with logic. Often, it is only through time and reflection that we can understand how an experience has changed and / or altered the manner in which we see a situation or individual.

The Role of Storytelling in Human Experiences

Storytelling has been part of the human experience since 'people' began communicating and it is a method used to convey information and experience as well as be entertaining. Earliest myths were all oral and then people began to write down stories so they weren't lost in time. From this, various theories have developed around storytelling and one is the 'monomyth', which is a template across cultures for storytelling. Let's have a look at this below.

'In narratology and comparative mythology, the monomyth, or the hero's journey, is the common template of a broad category of tales that involve a hero who goes on an adventure, and in a decisive crisis wins a victory, and then comes home changed or transformed.

The concept was introduced in *The Hero with a Thousand Faces* (1949) by Joseph Campbell, who described the basic narrative pattern as follows:

> "A hero ventures forth from the world of common day into a region of supernatural wonder: fabulous forces are there encountered and a decisive victory is won: the hero comes back from this mysterious adventure with the power to bestow boons on his fellow man."

Campbell and other scholars, such as Erich Neumann, describe narratives of Gautama Buddha, Moses, and Christ in terms of the monomyth. Critics argue that the concept is too broad or general to be of much use in comparative mythology. Others say that the hero's journey is only a part of the monomyth; the other part is a sort of different form, or colour, of the hero's journey.

https://en.wikipedia.org/wiki/Hero%27s_journey

Storytelling in History and its Purpose in Human Experience

Storytelling in oral form was accompanied by some theatrics to make the stories as entertaining as possible. Many of the early narratives were based upon religious ceremonies and stories of the creation of the earth and people(s). As time moved on, these stories were accompanied by dance, music and/or theatre and often were part of lengthy rituals, often taking days. These stories were designed to bring meaning to people's lives by explaining their own existence and the purpose/meaning of life in a time when life expectancy was short and entertainment was scarce. Of course stories were also recorded as these experiences were significant to all people and these stories run across all cultures. Before writing, stories were recorded in pictures such as cave art, in tattoo designs on skin and in designs such as rock piles and the giant carved heads of Easter Island.

Writing changed the manner in which stories were told and many of the old oral traditions were lost, barely being kept alive by specialists. Stories began to travel across cultural and national boundaries on whatever surface could be created. Papyrus, bones, pottery, skins, paper and in more modern times film, video and digital storage have changed, over time, the way in which stories of human experience have been told and shared. Content evolved from myth, fable and legend to history, personal narratives and commentary. Modern narrative form often has an educational or didactic element and can drift into propaganda. Stories of self-revelation can be instructive and give audiences the opportunity to apply learning to individual lives, whereas historically narrative was used in this way for societies and groups as a whole. In recent times narratives have become interactive and audiences can choose how the narrative unfolds.

Whatever form the story takes we all have a seemingly innate need for narratives to make sense of our lives. They either confirm our world view or alter our world view depending on the experience they convey and the experiences that we bring to the narrative. We need to remember that narratives are important to human experience and have been significant since the beginning of time.

The Text as an Experience

The concept of the text as an experience is one area to consider as we look at *Texts and Human Experiences*. Reading or viewing the text is an experience in itself and when we do this we bring our own history (experiences) to the text and this helps shape our understanding.

Think about the personal perspective that you bring to a text. What are some of your experiences that might influence how you read a particular text? Some texts, especially personal narratives of trial and tribulation or loss, can be confronting to some audiences and bring back strong opinions or emotions. Many texts attempt to do this as they convey a particular point of view about the world.

Does what you bring to the text affect what you learn from that text? We also need to delve into how the narrative experience is conveyed and how this in turn impacts upon the manner in which the story is received by audiences across different cultures. For example, Western films where heroes fight Islamic terrorism may well be viewed very differently by audiences in Western democracies and Islamic countries. Even seemingly innocuous narratives like the movie 'The Red Pill' which is about men's rights and created by a woman, has caused a polarisation of views wherever it has been shown. Strong personal experiences and viewpoints certainly bring their own understandings to texts.

Questions for Texts and Human Experiences

- Define the module in your own words.
- How are people connected by shared experiences?
- How might physical experience(s) change the way you respond to the world?
- How do you think a person's context and prior experiences shape how they perceive the world?
- Are experiences unique or do prior experiences have an impact on a current experience and way of seeing life?
- What is positive about human experiences?
- Discuss what is negative about human experiences.
- To what extent does experience shape the way we see other people and / or groups?
- Is an individual's culture part of their experience or is it something else?
- Is it possible not to have any meaningful experiences at all?
- Why do people tell stories?
- What do you think you might learn from a narrative?

STUDYING FILM

Film provides us with a source of entertainment, even escapism, on a daily basis. Although many films can be enjoyed and interpreted with little effort on our part, others operate on more than one level. As well as being entertaining, they have a message for the responder. They tell us something about our world or ourselves.

In order to achieve this level of interpretation, it is essential to consider how film techniques and conventions, the tools of the filmmaker, have been used to make meaning.

We are able to enjoy and understand films every day because we have an implicit understanding of the basic techniques and conventions upon which a film text relies. For instance, we know that when the camera moves in on a sleeping person's face and the sound becomes distorted and echoing that we are about to see a dream sequence.

Studying film requires you to develop a critical awareness of such conventions and the technical language, or jargon, required to label and discuss the various components of film and how they are used by the filmmaker to convey a particular message. The glossary included in this guide provides a basic overview of the terminology required for the study of film as text at HSC level.

It is important to consider that the construction of meaning in film is not accidental, but the result of careful planning. An individual scene in a screenplay will be made up of dozens of individual shots, edited from a much larger amount of raw film footage. In the creation of a shot, the filmmaker considers five variables: shot size, framing, focus, angle and movement. These are the aspects of film language that need to be considered in your analysis and will be discussed in the analysis section of this guide.

In addition, the director gives careful consideration to how each shot is composed. This is called mise-en-scene. Mise-en-scene refers to everything else that happens in a shot, apart from the main action. Analysing this involves looking at elements like setting, costume, lighting and the movements of the other actors in the scene. For instance, costume can be used to convey the social status or personality of a character, lighting can be used to enhance a particular mood or the actions of the main character may be compared to the actions of other characters in the background of the scene.

The use of sound in a film, including voices, sound effects and the musical score is also an essential consideration.

Soundtracks in films are used in two ways. Firstly they include the sounds that we would expect to hear, such as dialogue and realistic sounds like a door closing or the noise of an approaching car. This is called *diagetic* sound because it is part of the narrative. Secondly, the soundtrack includes sounds that are added to the film to create or suggest certain attitudes or effects – well known songs or an original score may be included to invoke a particular mood or attitude. Exaggerated sound effects and voiceovers are other examples. This soundtrack is called *non-diagetic* sound. Notably, silence is often used as an effective technique and must be considered as part of the soundtrack.

Finally, it is important to consider the style of the film you are studying, as certain conventions are associated with particular styles and genres of film. *Billy Elliot* is an example of dance drama which combines the elements of the drama genre and dance which separates it from the usual dramatic forms. Events are presented to the viewer, as an observer, in a realistic way. The real world setting, character development and conflict are based on a real world situation, in this case the coal miner's strike in Britain during 1984-5.

Steps to follow in the study of a film:

1.   Watch the film from beginning to end without interruption, preferably in one sitting.

2.   Record your first impressions of the film.

3.   Review each sequence of the film, making detailed notes about how the various components of the film have been used by the filmmaker.

4.   Looking at your detailed notes, decide how particular film techniques are used to explore the themes of the film and how these relate to the concept of Into the World.

5.   Create links between the film you have studied and other pieces of related material. Identify similarities and/or differences in terms of the message of the text and/or the language techniques that have been used to convey this message.

6.   Tie your ideas together in an extended piece of writing.

GENERAL GLOSSARY OF FILM TERMS

aerial shot

A shot taken from above the scene, usually an exterior shot.

camera angle

The position of the camera in relation to the subject. A shot may be taken from a low-angle, high-angle or eye-level. Different meanings are associated with different camera angles. For e.g. a low angle shot implies power.

close-up (CU)

A shot where the camera, and therefore the audience, is close to the subject e.g. when the head and shoulders of a character fill the screen.

cut

The juxtaposition and joining together of different shots, through editing, in the finished film.

editing

The joining of shots together, by cutting and arranging, to form a sequence. Rapid editing occurs when the sequence has many frames. This can create a sense of panic or urgency.

epic

A heroic tale, usually historical.

establishing shot

The initial shot of a scene, usually from a distance (aerial shot, long shot) showing the viewer where the action is about to occur.

extreme close-up

A shot where the camera is extremely close to the subject, for instance a shot of the eye of an actor only.

extreme long-shot

A shot, usually of an exterior location, taken from a long distance. Usually panoramic.

eye-level shot

Camera viewpoint which represents the view of an observer.

fast motion

A shot in which time is distorted by quickening the pace of the scene.

first person

See point of view shot.

foreground

The part of the shot or scene closest to the viewer, often in front of the action.

foregrounding

Bringing anything to the front, or foreground, of a scene.

genre

Common types or categories of film that are characterised by particular conventions e.g. romantic comedy, action adventure and science fiction are recognisable genres.

insert shot

A shot inserted into a sequence of shots, during editing, to create emphasis. Usually a close-up showing detail.

jump cut

An abrupt but deliberate transition between shots.

long shot (LS)

A shot where the camera is a long way from the subject.

low-angle shot

A shot where the camera is below the subject.

medium shot

A relatively close-up shot of a subject. For instance most of a human figure is evident.

mise-en-scène

The various elements that make up the background of the scene.

montage

A series of shots, rapidly edited together to show the passing of time.

narration

A speaking voice, either from a character on-screen or an off-screen voiceover, that provides commentary on the action or plot.

pan

Also a panning shot, a shot that moves the camera to encompass the full width of a scene.

parallel action

The use of cross-cutting to present multiple stories at the one time.

point of view shot(POV)

A shot that shows the viewer what the character in the film sees.

rapid cutting

A style of editing that juxtaposes short sharp scenes in a sequence.

realism

A genre of film in which authentic locations and details are used to portray reality.

re-establishing shot

Usually follows closer shots, allowing the viewer to recover a sense of the context of the scene.

reverse angle-shot

After one shot the camera turns around to show the same shot from the opposite direction.

scene

An incident in the action, composed of a series of separate but related shots.

score

The background music, separate from the sound track.

screen-play

The written version of the film, including dialogue, description of the action and, sometimes, directions for the camera.

segue

Use of a device to link one scene to another e.g. a voiceover.

sequence

A series of scenes.

shot

A length of film taken without stopping.

slow motion

A shot in which time is distorted by slowing down the action in the scene.

sound

All recorded music, dialogue and background noise. Also the use of silence.

sound track

All of the sound recorded in a film, including the score. (Diegetic sound is the internal sound of the film. Non-diegetic sound is the super-imposed sound placed over and into the film.

symbol

An object or event that represents something else and has meaning beyond the literal.

voiceover

Dialogue spoken off-screen.

wide-shot

A shot taken from a distance, including the entire setting where the action takes place.

zoom

To make the subject appear to approach (zoom-in) or recede (zoom-out) from the camera/viewer.

THE DIRECTOR – STEPHEN DALDRY

The role of the director is to interpret the screenplay in order to create the final product that appears on the screen. Although the director is in charge of the overall vision of the film, they will still work in conjunction with a production crew. This process may involve the interpretation of the characters, production design and the composition of the frame.

Billy Elliot was the director, Stephen Daldry's first major feature film; a transition made from a successful 15-year career in the theatre. Daldry is the son of singer and bank manager who first developed his talent for the stage as an apprentice to the Italian clown, Elder Molletti and as a member of a youth drama group in Taunton England.

After establishing his directorial work by being part of the Crucible Theatre in Sheffield from 1985 to 1988, Daldry travelled to London to direct over 100 plays as part of the fringe theatre, the Gate. He converted this small fringe theatre to suit a more international audience, receiving recognition and accolades for his work. The visionary production and deconstructionist staging of J. B Priestly's *An Inspector Calls*, received a Tony Award when the production transferred to Broadway.

At the age of 32, he was appointed the director of the Royal Court where he held the position of the artistic director from 1992 to 1995. This was a phenomenal effort from a man who was educated at Sheffield University and has a background in radical politics. In the 80s Daldry was a member of Sheffield University Socialist Worker's Party. There, he developed his own political beliefs and knowledge that has influenced his productions in the theatre and on film. *An Inspector Calls* can be explored as a critique of Margaret Thatcher's, Britain. Thatcher was the Conservative Prime Minister of Britain from 1979–90.

During this time Daldry was approached by the film production company Working Title to develop a career in film. He first directed the short film *Eight* (1998), followed by *Billy Elliot*, which was originally titled *Dancer*. Working Title is also responsible for other British films such as *Notting Hill* (1999), *Elizabeth* (1998), *Four Weddings and a Funeral* (1994) and the more recent *Love Actually* (2003).

Another aspect of Daldry's personal context that has influenced *Billy Elliot* is the death of his father from cancer, when he was 14. Daldry worked his own emotions into Billy who has also permanently lost his mother.

Daldry's recent productions include *The Hours* (2002) staring Nicole Kidman, Meryl Streep and Julian Moore which is an adaptation of Michael Cunningham's novel which is itself a derivative of Virginia Woolf's *Mrs Dalloway*. In 2008 he worked on *The Reader*, in 2011 *Extremely Loud and Incredibly Close* and *Trash* in 2014. He has a production called *Wicked* planned for 2019.

BILLY ELLIOT

Inside every one of us is
a special talent waiting
to come out

The trick is finding it

SCENE NAMES

1. Main titles
2. A Disgrace in the Gloves
3. The Ballet Class
4. To Be a Dancer
5. Dad Finds Out
6. Mrs Wilkinson's Offer
7. Private Lessons
8. A Ghost Story
9. Tony's Arrest
10. The Chance to Dance
11. Christmas
12. A Dance of Defiance
13. Dad's Decision
14. The Audition
15. The Interview
16. The Letter
17. Billy's Big Night
18. End Titles

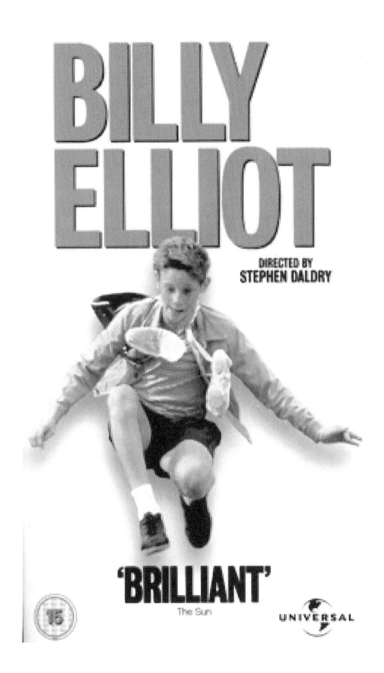

CHARACTER AND CAST NAMES

FOR BILLY ELLIOT – UNIVERSAL (2000)
(105 minutes)
Rated M

Jamie Bell............................	Billy Elliot
Gary Lewis............................	Dad/ Jacky Elliot
Julie Walters........................	Mrs Wilkinson
Jamie Draven........................	Tony Elliot
Jean Heywood.......................	Grandma
Stuart Wells.........................	Michael Caffrey
Nicola Blackwell....................	Debbie Wilkinson
Mike Elliot...........................	George Watson
Janine Birkett.......................	Billy's Mum
Billy Fane............................	Mr Braithwaite
Adam Cooper.........................	Billy Elliot at age 25
Carol Mc Guigan.....................	The Librarian
Joe Renton...........................	Gary Poulson
Colin Mac Lachlan..................	Mr Tom Wilkinson
Trevor Fox............................	P C Jeff Peverly
Charlie Hardwick....................	Sheila Briggs

Stephen Daldry.......................	Director
Greg Brenman	Producers
Jon Finn	
David M Thompson	Executive Producers
Natasha Wharton	
Charles Brand	
Tessa Ross	
Lee Hall	Writer
Brian Tufano.........................	Cinematography

PLOT OUTLINE

Jacky and Tony are miners who are out on strike

Billy Elliot lives with his father Jacky, brother Tony and grandmother

Billy's interest in ballet develops

Billy is unsuccessful at boxing lessons

Billy is afraid that only "poofs" do ballet

Billy takes part in his first ballet lesson

Billy's dad finds out about the lessons

Debbie persuades Billy that dancers are as fit as athletes

Mrs Wilkinson tells Billy that he is good enough for the Royal Ballet School

Mrs Wilkinson offers Billy private lessons

The Elliot family find out about Billy's dream

Tony is arrested by the police, Billy misses out on the Newcastle audition

Jacky Elliot crosses the picket line for Billy

Billy dances for his father at Christmas in an act of defiance

The audition and interview

Jacky sells his deceased wife's jewellery to pay the fare to London

Billy becomes a successful Ballet Dancer

Billy is accepted into the Royal Ballet School

PLOT SUMMARY AND ANALYSIS

MAIN TITLES

Summary

The movie begins with an unidentified figure placing a record on a turntable that is centrally positioned in the frame. The song 'Cosmic Dancer' by T-Rex begins to play diagetically as the shot reveals a young adolescent male jumping on the bed to the music in slow motion. We assume that the boy is the protagonist of the film, Billy Elliot. The boy seems to be enjoying the experience, which is seen in the various gestures, and facial expressions that he is making.

The shot cuts to a long shot of Billy jumping on the bed as the title of the film appears. The scene progresses to have Billy getting breakfast ready with the music now acting non-diagetically as part of the sound track. His behaviour is typical of a boy his age, catching the toast with his plate, opening the sliding doors with his head. The person who he is fixing breakfast for is gone Billy runs out of the house to find his grandmother in a nearby park. Above the park are police getting out of vans, getting their riot gear ready in their daily assignment of controlling the violence of the striking miners.

The music ends in the next shot when Billy is in bed. Tony, Billy's brother accuses Billy of playing his records.

The shot cuts to the next day where Billy is now seated at the piano. Tony and Billy's father Jacky are getting ready to join the picket line. Jacky Elliot disapproves of Billy playing the piano.

Billy's response is that "Mum would have let us". The camera tilts up to focus on photographs of Billy's mother. From this scene we gather that Billy's mother has recently passed away.

Analysis

The beginning scene introduces us to the Elliot family and orientates us to where is film is set. The protagonist, Billy is a typical adolescent boy growing up in a working class family in the North-west of England. His actions show that he likes to have fun and joke around but he is also responsible to his family with a duty to look after his Grandmother who displays features of dementia.

The opening sequence also established the setting of the film, in other words this is the specific situation that we are to examine. Billy Elliot is a young boy growing up in Everington, Country Durham with his father Jacky, older brother Tony and grandmother during the strike of 1984.

From this scene we are also told that music is an important feature of the film. The music chosen to accompany this scene matches a central theme of the film, which is dance and the freedom of expression that it brings. At the beginning of the film, the music belongs to Billy's brother Tony who does not allow him to touch his music and the piano that Billy's father does not want him to play. A nostalgic soundtrack is also used to allude to the memories of Billy's mother.

Questions

1. Music plays an important role in Billy Elliot. How does music shape our response to the film? Think about how music links to the human experience.

2. The music of T-Rex plays and important role in supporting the narrative. Using the Internet and other resources, research the context of this rock group.

3. Evaluate how Jamie Bell's facial expressions and body language establish Billy's personality.

4. Use the table on the following page to guide your analysis of Billy Elliot. Remember that not all of the characters move into the world. You can compare the characters that experience change with those that don't.

WHO is the Character?	WHAT is their context?	WHY do they move?	WHERE are they going?	HOW is this represented?
BILLY				
JACKY				
TONY				
MRS WILKINSON				
MICHAEL				

A DISGRACE IN THE GLOVES

Summary

The scene begins with an establishment shot of the violence of the picket line. Tony is in the midst of the action yelling abuse at the police officers. The shot cuts to a long shot of Billy outside the boxing studio talking to his best friend Michael. As they talk, other boys push past Billy to get inside. From their discussion, we find that Billy is not good at boxing and that the old gloves he is using that "went out with the ark" belong to his father.

When Billy enters the boxing club in the next shot, the class has already started. He enters the ring to start sparring with another boy of the same age. As the bell for the beginning of the round sounds, so does the piano for the ballet lesson. The ballet lesson is taking place in the bottom half of the boxing hall as downstairs, where the lessons are usually held, is being used for a soup kitchen for the striking miners.

Instead of boxing properly, Billy begins to act childishly to the music. It seems as if he does not want to hit his opponent and is using this behaviour to compensate for his lack of boxing talent. From George Watson, the boxing coach's reaction we gather that Billy has acted like this before in the ring.

The scene progresses to the point-of-view of the boys sparring in a shot-reverse-shot transition. Jacky Elliot is watching from the sidelines. Jacky yells to Billy to hit the other boy but ironically Billy is distracted and is subsequently knocked to the floor by his opponent.

George tells Billy "Jesus Christ Billy Elliot, you're a disgrace to them gloves, your father and the traditions of this boxing hall..."

Analysis

From this scene we gather that boxing is a tradition not only for the males in the Elliot family but for the wider community as well. It is expected that Billy should take this sport seriously. A negative attitude towards dance especially ballet is established in this scene by the dialogue. George Watson tells Billy that it "is man to man combat, not a bloody... dance". A common belief is presented that to be masculine is to play a 'real' sport.

This scene is also building the framework of the complication that will develop for Billy as he makes his transition to become an adult. Billy is part of the world of mining and boxing. It is expected that this is the world that he will stay in and not seek new experiences outside this well-defined role.

Questions

1. Compose an Information Report on the 1984 miners' strike.

2. Why are traditions important? Describe some of your family's traditions.

3. The human experience is based in tradition but that is not enough: we need new experiences. Think about this idea as you watch the film. Is this a reasonable statement?

THE BALLET CLASS

Summary

Billy is at the punching bag where he is told to remain until he does it properly. He has been given the responsibility to give the keys to Mrs Wilkinson when he has finished. Billy soon loses interest in the bag. The shot cuts to a subjective point-of-view shot from Billy observing Mrs Wilkinson and the piano accompanist Mr Braithwaite. This technique enables the responder to view the events from Billy's position, which creates identification with the protagonist. Mrs Wilkinson is smoking and is not really concentrating on the girls undertaking the lesson.

As the shot cuts back to Billy, he begins to move in time to the music and the swaying of the punching bag. It seems as if Mrs Wilkinson's instructions for her lesson are also meant for him. Billy begins to punch the bag rhythmically to the music and the count that Mrs Wilkinson is providing. As Billy's interest in the lesson becomes obvious, a flute sounds in the non-diagetic soundtrack.

In the next shot Billy seems to be observing the lesson with the girls dancing in the foreground. Rather it is Billy's reflection that is seen in the frame. As the girls move into the centre the shot size becomes a medium long shot of Billy's reflection trapped with the frame of the mirror and the real Billy who is trying to give the smoking Mrs Wilkinson the keys. Billy is asked by Debbie, the daughter of Mrs Wilkinson, to join the lesson but Billy's response is "no." Amusingly the next shot is a tracking shot of the girls practising their steps and Billy is in the midst of them copying the move. The close up of the ballet slippers is juxtaposed with Billy's blue boxing boots.

In the centre of the room at the barre, the dancers are now performing side leg raises. Mrs Wilkinson begins to walk down the middle of the dancers and tells the dancers hold the movement. She notices Billy's natural talent for ballet and the pointed arch in his foot. Billy displays "a nice straight leg with good arch." The class is dismissed.

On the way home Mrs Wilkinson and Debbie pull up alongside Billy to ask him for the 50p for that lesson. Billy's response is that he does not owe her anything. Mrs Wilkinson asks Billy whether he enjoyed it but he does not answer. They drive off leaving Billy in the middle of the road. 'Top Hat White Tie and Tails' performed by Fred Astaire begins to play in the background acting as a segue to the next shot which is the source of soundtrack; an excerpt of the movie *Top Hat* (1935).

The scene moves in another direction with a dissolve to an extreme long shot of Billy and his grandmother walking across the horizon. The setting of the green grass of the cemetery is juxtaposed with the harsh industrial buildings and factories in the background. Billy's grandmother is telling Billy about the time when she was young and his mother was a girl; they would go to the Palace Picture house to watch movies and dance in front of the theatre like "lunatics". Fred Astaire was his mother's favorite. A medium long shot of Billy's grandmother framed by two chimneys precedes her statement that she could have been a professional dancer.

At his mother's grave, Billy throws alcohol cans away and attempts to clean the graffiti off the headstone. He even trims the grass with scissors that he has brought with him. The piano refrain symbolic of Billy's mother is heard in the soundtrack. According to the tombstone, Billy's mother dies less than a year earlier at age 38. The grandmother is at the wrong grave. The scene ends at night when Billy is about to go to sleep. He asks his brother if he ever thinks about death but he is met with a curt reply.

Analysis

The scene presents Billy's growing attraction to dance and the natural gift that he has for ballet. At this stage in the film, Billy is confused about what he should do, boxing or ballet? He enjoyed the class but he is also aware of what his family would think. It is as if he is split in two. The framing used within the scene represents this. The reflection of Billy trapped by the frame of the mirror is symbolic of his growing up and developing interest in dance. Billy is confined to the expectations of his social and cultural context. Billy wants to take his first step into the world but is confused about how he should make those steps.

Questions

1. How do we know that Billy enjoyed the experience of the lesson?

2. Describe how the features of shot sizes and camera angles make Billy stand out in the lesson?

3. List your first impressions of Mrs Wilkinson.

4. Fred Astaire is a popular dance figure of the classic films of Hollywood. He has been hailed as the greatest dancer to ever have graced the silver screen has genius, grace personified and simply the best dancer ever. Explain the symbolism of the excerpt from *Top Hat*.

5. Why is it important to know that Billy's grandmother could have been a professional dancer?

TO BE A DANCER

Summary

The scene begins with a tracking shot of Debbie and Billy walking down the street in their school uniforms. Debbie is dragging a stick along the brick wall and the prominently displayed 'Strike Now' posters that are plastered all over them. Sirens can be heard on the distance. They walk past riot police and Debbie continues to drag her stick across their shields as if it was a normal everyday occurrence or as if the police were not there. Debbie is encouraging Billy to continue with the lessons. She is trying to convince Billy that all male ballet dancers are not "poofs" but are in fact fit athletes.

Billy and Debbie pause in a long shot in front of a billboard. Half of the advertisement is not there. Ironically the image is of a Servis washing machine with a typical masculine figure positioned as if he is coming out of the frontloading washing machine. The text on the advertisement reads, "your ever- faithful washday slave" suggesting that the man as well as the washing machine are slaves.

The scene quickly changes to Billy at the piano, then Billy in the change rooms as he is sneaking in to the ballet lesson. In the lesson he finds himself lost in the dance moves and is told to follow the others. At the end of the lesson Mrs Wilkinson asks Billy if he will continue to attend the class next week. Billy's response is that he feels like a "right sissy". Mrs Wilkinson replies, "then don't act like one."

The next shot is of Billy at home hiding his ballet shoes underneath his mattress. He is almost caught by his father who reinforces the belief that boxing is a masculine tradition as the boxing gloves were his fathers.

The song 'Get It On' by T-Rex plays on the soundtrack as the scene moves to Billy at school. In a Physical Education class with Michael, they are undertaking a cross-country run. Michael takes Billy on a short cut where he then asks Billy about the ballet lessons. Michael asks Billy if he gets to wear a tutu. Billy's response is that tutus are for girls and that he just wears his shorts. Michael suggests that Billy would look "wicked" in a tutu. They continue to run.

The next shot is of Billy going to the mobile Durham County library. Billy is looking at book on ballet but is told that he can't borrow it on a junior ticket. While the librarian is distracted Billy commits his own piece of mischief as he steals the book. Using the book Billy practices the first arabesque in the bathroom. This is contrasted with the parallel scenes of Billy performing the same movement in his bedroom and the lessons. Billy finally has success as a dancer and he dances all the way home, a positive experience that shows how he has changed his attitude.

Analysis

This scene explores various issues relating to gender. Gender is more than just the differences between male and female. A person's gender is constructed by society's expectations about how to act as a female and a male. Billy assumes that all ballet dancers are homosexuals which is a belief shared by his family and wider community because of their limited experiences. Debbie tells him otherwise, that real men do dance and are in fact as fit as athletes.

Throughout this scene Billy is contemplating whether he should move into the world of dance but he is aware of his father's reaction.

The advertisement in the background suggests that females and males are not limited to their stereotypical gender roles. Males can do the washing just as well as they can dance. When Billy is feeling silly about his performance as a dancer, he is told not to act like a sissy. Billy's behaviour reflects a conflict between his community's expectation of male behaviour and his desire to participate in dance, which fits in with the female stereotype. His friend Michael, who is experimenting with his sexual identity, seems unaffected by the expectations of his community.

Questions

1. How does this scene present the idea that the strike has become a normal part of life for the community? For example the shot where Debbie and Billy walk past the riot police without noticing them.

2. How would you rephrase the meaning of gender?

3. What part of the dialogue supports the concept that gender is more than the difference between being male and female, it is also about human experiences?

4. What is the relationship between the various posters and billboards that are presented as part of the mise-en-scene and the plot?

DAD FINDS OUT

Summary

The scene commences back at the picket line. The boxing trainer George Watson is telling Jacky Elliot that he hasn't seen Billy or Jacky for months. As the bus crosses the picket line the violence and anger of the striking miners erupts. The aerial shot of the picket line is contrasted with the power and grace of Billy's dance moves. Now it seems that Mrs Wilkinson's instructions are also commenting on Jacky on the picket line.

When Billy is sneaking out to a lesson, a news radio broadcast of Margaret Thatcher is playing in the background. The radio announcer says, "In a speech to Tory M.P's yesterday, Prime Minister Margaret Thatcher referred to members of the striking National Union of Mine Workers as the 'enemy within'." Billy walks through a number of police to get to the lesson. In the middle of the lesson, Jacky arrives and orders Billy out.

Now at home, Jacky is arguing with Billy about what is wrong with ballet. Billy sees that there is nothing wrong with ballet but his father's response is that ballet is for girls "not for lads Billy, lads do football, boxing or wrestling. Not frigging ballet." The shot changes to a close up of Billy's face as he responds to his father's words. Father and son end in a scuffle where Billy leaves the house in anger and frustration. The 'Children of the Revolution' soundtrack by T-Rex is reprised as Billy runs away and takes his anger out on another "Strike Now' poster.

The scene cuts to Billy now in school uniform walking through a middle class suburb that contrasts to his own. The setting of the houses is not cramped together and have lawns with cars parked out the front. Billy arrives at the Wilkinson's where he informs Mrs Wilkinson that his father won't allow him to attend class anymore. Billy stays for tea, during which we find out that the Wilkinson's have problems of their own. Mr Wilkinson is also out of work. From his middle class viewpoint, we are also provided with more information about the context of the miners' strike.

Throughout this scene we also observe Billy and Debbie's relationship develop. Debbie seems to know more about her parents than what they think.

Analysis

The scene clearly establishes the belief systems held by Jacky Elliot and the wider working class Durham community. Boys do not do ballet; rather they follow sports that are more 'masculine'. Not only is Billy restricted by the gender expectations of his society; he is also constricted by the socio-economic situation that the miner's strike puts his family in. Both these things are limiting to his life experiences. Billy also has to overcome the economic situation that the strike has placed his family in. The scene also establishes Jacky's character who struggles to give Billy the 50 p each week, let alone provide food for his family. What we need to focus on now is how the film represents Billy and his family's reaction to these challenges.

Jacky Elliot finding out about his son's dancing places another restriction on Billy's world. The reference to the striking miners as the "enemy within" may also be relevant to Jacky's function in becoming an obstacle in Billy's desire to lead his own life.

Questions

1. Who is Margaret Thatcher? Composes a feature article that explores Margaret Thatcher's England and her political beliefs.

2. What is the function of the radio excerpt that refers to Margaret Thatcher?

3. Evaluate the similarities and differences between the action on the picket line and the ballet lesson.

4. Why is the framing of Mrs Wilkinson's street different to that of Billy's neighbourhood? Is setting and home life relevant to human experiences?

MRS WILKINSON'S OFFER

Summary

As Mrs Wilkinson is dropping Billy off at the corner, she tells Billy of her intention to try him out for the Royal Ballet School. Mrs Wilkinson reassures him by telling him that they are interested in potential "...it is how you move and express yourself that is important." Mrs Wilkinson offers to tutor him privately, without payment, and without his father knowing.

The scene shifts as Billy arrives at Michael's house. Michael is dressing up in his sister's clothes and is putting make up on. When Billy asks him if he'll get into trouble if anyone sees him, Michael says they won't. During their conversation we realise that Michael's father also dresses in female clothes. Michael puts lipstick on Billy. Billy asks Michael the question, "Do you think being a ballet dancer would be better than being a man?"

Billy talks to Michael about the idea of ballet school and the consequences of telling his father.

Analysis

From this scene we see the relationship between Billy and Mrs Wilkinson develop. They talk and argue with each other as equals, rather than teacher and student. Not only is Billy expressing doubt in his own ability but also he is also afraid of the consequences if his father found out about the private lessons.

The concept of gender is further explored at Michael's house. Billy is finding freedom and self- expression through dance but it is Michael who is experimenting with his sexuality by dressing in female clothes. How do you see this scene as an experience for the boys?

PRIVATE LESSONS

Summary

This scene is Billy's first private lesson where he has brought special things with him for inspiration for a dance he would use for his audition. Billy's shadow first enters the frame, followed by a long shot of the real Billy walking into the boxing hall. The scene cuts to another long shot but this time it is from Billy's point-of-view. The natural lighting highlights Mrs Wilkinson in the background of the frame.

One of the items that Billy has brought with him us a letter written to him by his mother. Mrs Wilkinson begins to read the letter out loud but Billy knows the letter of by heart and finishes it for her. An important piece of advice left for Billy is to "always be yourself". The piano soundtrack enhances the nostalgic atmosphere.

The following dance sequence is to the 'I Love to Boogie' tape, which is also performed by T-Rex. The shots of Mrs Wilkinson and Billy dancing to the energetic and upbeat music are contrasted with the parallel shots of the impact that this same music has in the Elliot home. Tony is in his bedroom using a carpet cleaner as a guitar, the grandmother is practising a ballet position and Jacky is having a bath.

The scene moves to early morning where Tony is sneaking out of the house. He wants to fight against the situation of hopelessness caused by the miner's strike. Jacky is also awake in anticipation of Tony's actions. In an intense dramatic episode, Jacky punches Tony in the face after his son yells at him saying that his father has not been a real man since the death of his mother. The tension is highlighted during a slow motion shot of Billy yelling, "Stop it," in reaction to the violent outburst.

The scene moves to Billy in the middle of another private lesson. The lesson is not going well. Billy is not landing a pirouette en dehors. Mrs Wilkinson's reaction is to tell Billy to concentrate but Billy just runs away to find solace in the change rooms. Mrs Wilkinson and Billy have a heated exchange of their own. The argument ends in a medium close up of Mrs Wilkinson comforting Billy. The next shot is a long shot of Billy practising the same pirouette movement but this time it is represented by the reflection in a mirror.

Analysis

From this moving scene we find out about the relationship that Billy had with his mother and the nurturing care that he is missing out on. It seems that Mrs Wilkinson is taking on the role of nurturer. Not only does Billy take is anguish out on her but he also turns to her for comfort.

Tony's character also develops in this scene. He is not one who will let the situation of the strike pass him by. He wants to be a man of action, even if these actions may be illegal.

Questions

1. Explain the symbolism of using Billy's shadow to enter the frame.

2. How does the use of lighting shape our feelings in this scene?

3. From the information presented in this scene, describe the relationship that Billy had with his mother. What emotional experiences is he missing because of her untimely death?

4. Discuss the symbolism of the special things that Billy has brought with him.

A GHOST STORY

Summary

This scene commences with an establishing shot of Billy and Mrs Wilkinson driving. Billy wants to play a tape and the music of *Swan Lake* beings to play in the background. Now on the ferry, Mrs Wilkinson recounts the story of the famous ballet *Swan Lake*. She says that the story of the young beautiful woman who is transformed into a swan and the prince who is the one thing that allows her to become human once more but he leaves her for another woman, resulting in the death of the beautiful young girl. Mrs Wilkinson said that this is only a ghost story. The setting of the mechanical docklands is juxtaposed with the beautiful soundtrack.

Billy is now in the kitchen at night. The camera pans to reveal the ghost of Billy's mother who tells him to not drink out of the bottle and to put the milk back into the fridge.

Billy is now rehearsing at the barre with Mrs Wilkinson. A tracking shot frames 360° of the graceful ballet movements. The scene changes to Billy who is now talking with Debbie. Debbie also does not want him to leave.

Analysis

The scene presents the idea of ghosts. A comparison can be made between the beautiful young girl of *Swan Lake* and Billy's mother who also died prematurely. Billy is also making progress in developing his ballet skills. The movements in this scene are graceful like a swan.

Questions

1. What is the function of ghosts in this scene?

TONY'S ARREST

Summary

The scene begins with a long shot of the riot police advancing on the strikers. Tony escapes into a house and the police give chase. The action of the scene is supported by the music of The Clash performing 'London Calling' in the soundtrack. The camera follows Tony as he runs through the houses in a jerking fashion. Tony humorously steals sips of tea and spits on a police car. Billy is watching the event from the fence of a nearby house. Tony is caught as he becomes tangled in washing drying on a clothesline.

Billy calls Mrs Wilkinson to say that he has a problem with the audition that is taking place tomorrow but it is Debbie who answers and she hangs up on him. The scene concludes with Mrs Wilkinson arriving the next day at the house.

Analysis

This short scene confirms the feeling of inequality between the miners and the government who are represented by the faceless police. The miners have little chance against the sheer number of police.

The community show their support for Tony as he runs through the various homes. The humour of this scene is short-lived by the prevailing sense of injustice where the police set upon the unarmed Tony.

Questions

1. How does the framing and editing techniques enhance the tension as Tony runs from the law? How does the audience perceive Tony's experience?

THE CHANCE TO DANCE

Summary

Tony, Jacky and Billy arrive home from the police station to the waiting Mrs Wilkinson. Mrs Wilkinson tells the Elliot family about Billy's audition for the Royal Ballet School. Tony is the most vocal in this scene expressing his disapproval of his brothers dancing but Billy actually verbally expresses his desire that he wants to be a dancer. Tony forces Billy to dance on the kitchen table to prove himself. The shot transfers to Billy's point-of-view so that the audience watching from his perspective of the argument between his family and Mrs Wilkinson. The shot is cut with a quick flash of Billy dancing outside to return to the argument between Tony and Mrs Wilkinson that is occurring inside. The argument is drowned out by the soundtrack, 'Town Called Malice' that was written by Paul Weller and performed by The Jam. When Mrs Wilkinson leaves, the scene moves to Billy who is in the back yard.

The scene transforms into a dance sequence where Billy is displaying his frustration and anger through a dance to the soundtrack. There is a long shot of Billy dancing into a brick wall in their backyard. He then runs his hands across the rough brick surface. Billy then kicks down the blue toilet door to continue to run through the backstreets of his neighbourhood to tap all the way down the empty street into a rusty cast iron wall. Michael calls Billy but the change in the setting to a snow filled street indicates that some time has passed.

Analysis

The scene explores the motif of Billy dancing into the wall symbolising the obstacles of his journey into a wider, experiental world. The wall represents the barriers that he is facing, those of gender expectations, family position and the financial situation that the strike has put him in. There is no break in the wall symbolising that he is trapped but there is hope. Billy kicks the blue toilet door down suggesting that these barriers can be transcended. He wants to kick the wall down but the events are beyond his control as an adolescent. The framing of this dance sequence not only allows Billy to display the stylised movements on his whole body but is also enhances the only feeling of freedom that he has while he dances.

It is not until Billy's family interferes in his decision to audition for the Royal Ballet School that he verbalises that this is what he wants to do for the rest of his life.

Questions

1. Explain the impact of the point-of-view shot from Billy's perspective.

2. How does the camera create the status of the characters using camera angles, shot size and dialogue?

3. Why do you think Jacky Elliot remains relatively silent during this scene?

4. How does the scene represent the development in Billy's relationship with his environment?

CHRISTMAS

Summary

The scene begins with the miners rallying together. George, the boxing coach, is leading a chorus of "Here we go." The scene changes to show Jacky cutting up the piano for firewood. The sound of the axe hitting the piano resonates to indicate the emotional impact that this act has on the family. Jacky beings to sob while Billy and the Grandmother are eating their Christmas meal.

The shot transitions to change to Billy and Michael who are making snowmen. During their discussion Billy tells Michael, "Just because I like ballet doesn't mean that I am a poof you know." Michael confides his sexuality to Billy.

Analysis

From this scene, we can tell that the family's financial situation has worsened. They do not have enough money to afford proper heating materials. Ironically most of the houses would have been heated by burning coal. The destruction of the piano is one less source of creativity that is within the Elliot household.

The theme of gender is also presented in this scene. Billy confirms his heterosexual status while Michael voices his homosexuality that has been alluded to in previous scenes. Billy is accepting of his best friend's transition into the world of his choice. This promotes the value of tolerance that is imbedded in the film's ideology. We should be more accepting about how others want to lead their lives and not assume that our experience is theirs.

Questions

1.   Why is it important to know that Billy is not gay in the context of the film and the experiences he is going through?

A DANCE OF DEFIANCE

Summary

Billy and Michael sneak into the boxing club. Billy gives Michael a tutu and teaches him some ballet positions. The drunken George observes the boys and runs to get the Jacky to come and see for himself. In an act of defiance, Billy dances the audition piece for his father to show him what he can do but Jacky just walks out. Michael claps uncomfortably. The strong rhythm and dynamics of the music match Billy's emotions and the pride that he has in his love for dance.

Analysis

The experience of the dance of defiance is a pivotal scene in Billy's journey into the adult world. It is in this scene that Jacky actually gets to see him dance and realise that his son has talent as a dancer. Billy is also not afraid to stand up to his father by spontaneously dancing for him. It is though this confrontation done by dance that Billy and his father grow closer together despite their differences.

This is a major step in Billy's transition. He is doing what he loves, despite what others think and the circumstances that may follow. The experience his father has in watching him dance is pivotal in their relationship and the resulting narrative.

Questions

1. Evaluate how the movements of Billy's dance are symbolic of his journey into the world. How does his father respond to the experience?

DAD'S DECISION

Summary

It is still Christmas, Jacky Elliot confronts Mrs Wilkinson about how much the audition will cost. He thanks her for all she has done for his son but tells her that because Billy is his son that he now needs to take responsibility.

The first decision that Jacky Elliot makes is to go back to work and cross the picket like so that he can afford to take Billy to London. As the bus crosses the picket line, Tony sees his father on the bus. The music soundtrack supports the emotions of the scene when Tony confronts his father. Jacky has gone against everything that the family has gone through and fought for as a result of the strike. Jacky breaks down and does not go through with going back to work. He then makes his next difficult decision, which is to pawn his wife's jewellery to pay for the trip to London. While Billy and Jacky are on the bus to the audition, we discover that this is also Jacky's first time to London. This is symbolic of how narrow their life experience has been and how this shapes attitudes towards the world.

Analysis

During this scene Jacky swallows his pride to give his son a chance. He has made his own journey to overcome his own misconceptions and established principles. It proves that despite his harsh exterior, Jacky does love his son and only wants the best for him. Jacky has also been confined by the expectation to be a miner. He has not had the opportunity to step out of his own community and fully experience life.

Questions

1. Why doesn't Jacky Elliot accept Mrs Wilkinson's offer to pay for the trip to London?

2. Who has the greater status in the conversation between Jacky and Mrs Wilkinson? How can we tell this from the film techniques used by the composer?

THE AUDITION

Summary

Jacky and Billy arrive in London. As they enter the Royal Ballet School the aerial long shot of Billy suggests that Billy is engulfed and overwhelmed by the situation. While waiting for the audition to begin, Billy seems to be overcome by nerves but Jacky reassures him and forces him back into the room. In the change rooms other boys are also preparing for their auditions. We overhear a young blonde boy's conversation with another boy who is auditioning. He says that this is his second audition. He then talks to Billy and asks him where he is from. Billy replies Durham County. The boy asks him about an amazing cathedral that is in that location but Billy has not seen it.

During the audition piece the medium long shots of the panel show a lack of an emotional response. When the audition ends,

Billy storms back into the change rooms despondent. Another young boy goes to Billy and attempts to comfort him. Billy is not used to the physical contact or sensitivity from an outsider let alone another male and reacts to the situation by punching the other boy and calling him a "bent bastard'.

Analysis

This is Billy's first time in the big city but from his conversation with the other boys who are auditioning we realise that Billy has not seen the sights of his own County. Durham County is in fact the site of England's finest Norman cathedrals that the young boy was talking about. Work on the cathedral began in 1093 and is considered to be one of the finest architectural achievements in the country. This information highlights how great the journey to London really is. On the other hand, Billy is faced with unfamiliar responses so he falls back onto the behaviour that he has learnt from his father and brother. This seems unusual for Billy given his friendship with Michael. This is Billy's big day, everything that he has been working towards but it seems that he is not able to deal with the pressure of his first and most important audition. The experience is overwhelming for him.

Questions

1. How do the film techniques portray Billy's emotions in this scene?

2. What would you say to defend Billy's actions in the locker room? How does Billy come to see the experience?

THE INTERVIEW

Summary

The scene begins with a long shot of Billy and Jacky sitting in the audition space. Again the framing suggests that the Elliots are overcome by the situation. The head member of the audition panel tells Billy and Jacky that Billy's actions may have negative consequences and that type of behaviour is not tolerated at their establishment. He proceeds to ask questions regarding Billy's interest in ballet. Billy's answers are not developed or substantial. The member of the audition panel asks Jacky whether he is a fan of the ballet and proceeds to explain the importance of having the total support of the family. This is the first time that we see Jacky verbalise the support that he has for his son. Jacky is also trying to make up for Billy's lack of answers to the interview questions.

The member of the audition panel then gives the Elliot's the opportunity to ask them any questions. As there aren't any, Jacky and Billy stand to leave. At that moment another female panel member asks Billy just one last question. She asks him what does it feel like when you are dancing? Billy's reply is, "Dunno, sort of feels good. Sort of safe ... but when I get going...I forget everything...um I sort of disappear, sort of disappear, I can feel a change in my whole body, just this fire in my body just there; like a bird, like electricity, yeah, like electricity."

The interview ends with the head panel member wishing the Elliot's well with the strike.

Analysis

The purpose of the interview is for the audition panel to gain an holistic impression of Billy and his family. Billy's answer to the final question is most interesting. His response describes the sensation of transformation through dance. By disappearing he is not only affected by the world and by saying that he feels a change, like a bird, expresses the freedom and liberation that dancing gives him. Fire and electricity connote the energy and power that he also feels while dancing.

The audition panel are also familiar with Billy's situational context and are aware of the effects of the miners' strike, which reinforces the fact that it is a national issue.

Questions

1. How do the film techniques used during the dance sequences portray Billy feeling like electricity?

2. Have a go at storyboarding one of the dance sequences. A storyboard is a way of mapping out what happens in a scene frame by frame. Be careful to pay attention to the framing and camera angles that are used to express the excitement of Billy dancing.

3. Describe the gestures and facial expressions that Jacky and Billy make that suggest that this world is a completely new experience for them.

THE LETTER

Summary

Jacky, Billy and Nan are sitting waiting. Nan tells Billy that he should get himself a trade, something useful. She reminds the family that she could have been a professional dancer. The shot changes to Billy at school in class with Michael. The post arrives in another shot with the letter. Billy arrives home with his family waiting for him at the kitchen table. Billy goes onto the next room to read the letter. The medium close of Billy's reaction to reading the letter does not confirm one way or another. As his family joins him, the crying Billy announces to them that he got in.

Jacky excitedly runs up the street. It is the same street that Billy had previously danced down. Jacky goes to tell his fellow miners the good news but is told that the union caved in, the strike is over and the miners are now going back. The shot cuts to Billy and Jacky at the cemetery. They are happy, laughing and joking around.

Billy goes to the hall where Mrs Wilkinson is giving a lesson to tell her the news but she already knows. She asks him, "Does this mean you will go out and find life and all those other things?" She wishes Billy well and continues with the lesson.

Billy quickly says goodbye to Michael as he leaves for the bus. While Billy is on the bus, Tony says that his will miss him but Billy cannot hear him. The scene shifts to Tony and Jacky who are back at work, Mrs Wilkinson who is alone in the boxing club then to Billy finally leaving on the bus. The scene concludes with a dissolve.

Analysis

Billy has of course successfully gained entry into the exclusive Royal Ballet School. It seems as if the hard work has paid off to allow Billy to make his transition and live happily ever after. Billy is in fact moving on, going into the world and finding life, his life. Not only is his family supportive of his decision to dance and are happier but the greater community was also looking out for the news of Billy receiving the letter. Jacky is laughing with his youngest son and Tony even expresses that he will miss his younger brother. The breadth of experiences in the film because of Billy's dancing have opened up a whole range of ideas and attitudes for the community as well as the family.

Although the news of Billy's success is positive, it is met with the disappointing news that the strike has been unsuccessful. Life returns back to normal for Jacky and Tony as they return to the life down the pits. They may have emotionally grown up in developing acceptance and support of Billy dancing but their lives have not really changed.

Mrs Wilkinson's life also returns back to normal. She remains in a loveless marriage, teaching the same ballet class. She may not have had the talent to be a professional dancer herself but she has been able to use the skills that she has to help Billy. Billy has made her life more meaningful, she has found hope in his potential but we do not know if she will make a greater effort in teaching her regular ballet classes. The life that Billy will go out and find is the life that she missed out on, the experiences she never had.

Questions

1.   Why do you think Billy waited to tell Mrs Wilkinson that he was accepted into the Royal Ballet School?

BILLY'S BIG NIGHT

Summary

The scene commences with the continuation of the dissolve of Jacky and Tony on an underground train. They alight to arrive at the Theatre Royale Haymarket to watch Billy's performance. Fourteen years has passed and Billy is now a professional dancer. Jacky and Tony are late and are hurriedly seated next to a grown up Michael and his partner. The performance begins starting with the music of *Swan Lake*. Jacky is overcome with emotion.

The shot changes to a medium close up of the back of the adult Billy about to get ready for his entrance. The lighting that is from above and in front of Billy surrounds him in a surreal glow. The music grows with the anticipation and Billy begins to warm up. The frame is a close up of Billy when he is told that his family is there. We assume from the music and dance costume that Billy has a main role in a performance of *Swan Lake*. The other chorus dancers are waiting for Billy to enter. The moment that we all have been waiting for begins as Billy leaps into the air in a triumphant move. The scene ends with Billy frozen in position.

Analysis

The scene is the culmination of Billy's efforts to make the most of his life experiences and not be confined as his father and brother are. He has grown up and has achieved success. Swan Lake is no longer a ghost story but is in fact a triumphant reality. The response that he made at the interview for the audition has come true. Not only the mise-en-scene of his costume is a bird but it also seems that he is literally filled with fire. Electricity is in the air in anticipation of Billy's entrance.

Michael has also grown up and is being true to himself. He has moved into his world despite what others may think of him. He too is happy.

Questions

1. What is Billy's final leap in the air symbolic of?

2. What is the function of the ballet *Swan Lake*?

3. Evaluate the film techniques that represent Billy's success.

END TITLES

Summary

The film ends where it began with Billy jumping on his bed to the song that says, "If I believe that I can do anything". In the background is the adult Billy performing the pirouettes that he found difficult but now completes perfectly.

Analysis

The final sequence reinforces the belief that if you put your mind to it, you can do anything. The film leaves us with images of the young Billy Elliot to remind us where he came from.

SETTING

Billy Elliot is located in the fictional Everington, a coastal pit village of Country Durham situated in Northern England. Everington is in fact the real mining village Easington. The film is set in 1984 amidst the context of Britain's worst industrial dispute in the country's post war history. Easington was ironically one of the biggest coal producing town in Europe before the strike. Many of the extras at the picket lines were real miners who actually went out on strike in 1984.

The year-long miners' strike had a tremendous impact on the Thatcher government and the economy. The conservative Thatcher government was unwilling to support what it saw as a failing industry for the long term. Tens of thousands of miners went on strike following an announcement that the "uneconomic" pits would have to close, putting 20 000 miners out of work.

The strike action was sidelined by the numerous violent confrontations at the picket lines and the hardships that were evident in the mining communities. Twenty years on, the impact of the strike remains. There were only 12 deep pits in the United Kingdom that still produced coal and three of those mines closed in 2004. In the end the biggest losers were the ordinary miners.

The film examines the relationships of the coal mining family struggling to come to terms with the impact of the strike; the film begins during the early stages of the strike and concludes a year later when the strike is over. The threat of the strike has produced a community that has become tightly knit but the end of mining would also result in the end of community.

Billy has come from a family with a strong mining and boxing tradition. It is expected that Billy would also become a miner and a boxer just like his father and his father's father. The miner's conflict is reflected in the conflicts in the smaller world of the Elliot household. Billy is facing his own struggle. Billy's mother has recently passed away leaving him in a male dominated household. On top of all this, Billy attempts to discover a means of expressing himself, which he eventually does through dance. The Elliot family is in crisis; the whole family is confused. The father is unsure of the outcome of the strike, Tony seems certain of absolute victory and Billy's grandmother is uncertain of anything leaving Billy caught in the middle of it all.

The mise-en-scene of the setting reflects the sense of Billy being closed in by his family's situation and the impact that the strike has on the community. The Elliot household is within a working class community. The houses are all cramped together with little or no greenery. The washing is hung in communally, and the toilets are outside. The tight framing enhances the notion that Billy is trapped by his context.

In comparison, the area where the Wilkinson's live are middle class; the families have cars that are parked outside on the lawns and the houses are not fenced in. The Director of Photography, Brian Tofano collaborated with Stephen Daldry to frame "the mining village in a claustrophobic way to reflect the tight knit community. The buildings were a part of the narrative, so we framed them tight and have them spilling outside of the framework.[1]"

---

1   http://www.billyelliot.com/pages/life.html

© Five Senses Education Pty Ltd

CHARACTER ANALYSIS

Billy Elliot

At 11 years of age, Billy is the youngest member of the Elliot household. He is coming to terms with life and the expectations of becoming a man. He has been forced to grow up quickly due to the death of his mother and the economic situation that the miner's strike has put his family in, both extremely negative experiences for Billy and the family. Billy is a mature person who also has the responsibility of looking after his grandmother. Billy is not only at odds with his family over his desire to become a dancer but he is also pitted against the community and the larger hostile world. Billy goes through a tough time but he embraces these experiences to make himself stronger.

Billy turns to dance as a means of artistic expression but it becomes more than that. Dance is also a means of liberation and freedom for Billy. Billy has a spark of something special, not only is this a natural gift for dance but he also has the determination to make his dream a reality. This determination also makes his character all the more likeable and we are empathetic to him as he has the variety of experiences that lead him to become a professional dancer.

The costumes that Billy wears reflect his status in the community. Apart from his school uniform, Billy wears the typical dress of an adolescent growing up in Northern England. When he is not wearing the singlets and shorts that he dances in, Billy is seen in worn and faded denim jeans and jacket. Jamie Bell's performance as Billy Elliot also parallels the character's context. This is an excellent feat for the first time actor who has been dancing since he was six years old. Jamie Bell was cast from the thousands of other boys who tried out for this role.

What is more interesting about the character are the many characteristics that both Billy and Jamie Bell share. Not only do they have the common gift for dance but are separately pushed to reach their full potential. Jamie was also confronted with the belief that dance is not for boys; it is more for girls. Jamie Bell even came from Billington, a village that is a dozen miles south to where the film is set. This means that Jamie Bell would speak in the same register as a young boy from Durham County.

Jamie Bell uses gestures and facial expressions to convey the emotions that Billy is going through. The facial expressions range from the joy and excitement on the opening titles of Billy jumping to one of his favourite rock song to the disappointment and frustration felt from his audition. These help convey the emotion of the experiences he has and allows us to vicariously share how he feels about each of these experiences. In the end the experiences are positive for Billy – he has overcome the negatives and is a professional dancer. We know his motivations which give him the power to overcome any of the negative experiences he faces.

Mrs Wilkinson

Mrs Wilkinson is an enduring figure who is rarely seen without a cigarette in hand while she barks out instructions to her class, which makes her character even more lasting. She has a daughter who is the same age as Billy but is also trapped within her middle class world. Mrs Wilkinson is in a loveless marriage where husband who has cheated on her has been made redundant and now spends most of his time drinking. The function of Mrs Wilkinson's character is important as she instrumental on Billy's journey as she gives him much of her experience as a dancer so that he can move on from his background and have new experiences.

Billy's relationship with is dance teacher is a key element in the film that develops as the film progresses. It is Mrs Wilkinson who dares Billy to wear the ballet slippers in the first place and it is she who recognises the talent that has the potential to progress to the Royal Ballet School. Once she knows that Billy does indeed have something special, she seems to become completely obsessed by it. It is obvious from Billy's visit to the Wilkinson household that Billy has been the topic of conversation.

Mrs Wilkinson does not treat Billy like a child; rather they bicker and argue like equals. She takes on a nurturing role as she helps him to fulfil his dreams to become a dancer. Mrs Wilkinson may have developed personally in her support for Billy but at the end of the film her circumstances have not changed. She does not go to see Billy's first major performance and her family situation is still the same as she continues to teach ballet to have a sense of fulfilment.

Mrs Wilkinson does not look like the typical ballet teacher. Her hair and clothes are messy, she chain smokes and she barks out the instructions to her students.

Jacky Elliot

Jacky is the strong patriarch of the family who holds onto traditional masculine values. Although he often turns to violence to solve problems, we should not forget that Jacky has also experienced horrendous changes with the recent death of his wife and the emasculating lack of employment. His world is changing around him but he does not have the emotional capacity to deal with it, these changes are outside his experience and he cannot cope.

Jacky is too caught up in his own insular world to realise that his son is sneaking out of the house to go to ballet lessons. He has to be told by George the boxing coach that his son is no longer turning up to boxing. He is hurt when he sees that his son is not going to be a boxer or a football player. Jacky becomes part of Billy's world once he realises the talent that his youngest son has. Jacky then takes on the responsibility to make Billy's dreams come true, whether it be the sacrifice of pride in crossing the picket line or selling his wife's jewellery. It is on the night of Billy's performance that we see Jacky Elliot stepping out and taking on new experiences, emotionally and physically.

Gary Lewis has been well cast to play the father who is coming to terms with his emotions. His body language portrays his stubborn nature but this is compared with the heart-felt emotion of chopping up his wife's piano for firewood at Christmas.

Tony Elliot

It is easy to forget that Tony is facing the same hardships of the loss of his mother and employment. Tony is a loud obnoxious character who selfishly verbalises his opposition to Billy's dancing. He appears to be selfish and care only about his world. Tony's world revolves around the action of the picket line. While confronting a scab miner in the supermarket he yells, "You never cross a picket line...we're all fucked if you forget that."

Tony has confidence in a positive outcome for the strike and is not afraid to take the situation into his own hands, even if it puts him in trouble with the law.

It is not until Tony sees the sacrifice that his father made when he crosses the picket line when Tony becomes supportive of Billy dancing. We also see another aspect of his character in this scene when he breaks down while comforting his father. It is at this moment we see Tony moving away from the world of the picket line, back to become the sympathetic son and take on new experiences.

Michael Caffrey

Although Michael is Billy's best friend his character also functions to contrast the gender implications of the Billy Elliot character. Michael's sexuality reinforces Billy's heterosexuality. Michael is not afraid of what others think of him, whether it is refusing to go to boxing with the rest of the lads or putting make up and dresses on at home. Michael clearly has made his own experiential change, which is evident at his appearance at Billy's big night, the performance that Michael would not miss for the world.

Michael is also developing a means of self-expression. He expresses his self freely through the dialogue or through the mise-en-scène. Michael is from the same world as Billy. He lives in the same tight knit community with closed in housing and wears a similar basic costume as Billy but we know his experience of life will be different.

THEMES

- Human Experiences
- Human Experiences through Dance and Music
- Human Experiences – Growing Up
- Human Experiences – Gender

Human Experiences

We see a number of challenging experiences in the film *Billy Elliot* each experience compounds into a larger experience leading to the final performance on stage a a professional dancer. We have already established much about the content and context of the film in terms of this Common Module but a quick recap here is vital to enable you to focus on the rubric in your response. There can be no doubt that the film was composed to provoke new ideas and challenge assumptions by examining the mining town and the stereotypes that flourished under such a closed society.

If we examine the rubric we can see the collective experiences can be ascribed to both the miners, their families and the local children but we can also glean individual experiences and reactions to these experiences, such as Billy's breakout and Michael's sexuality. The human qualities that are exhibited such as resilience and understanding provoke strong emotions, especially when we see the passion Billy has for dance, the struggle of the miners against overwhelming forces and the relationships within the family such as those between Billy and his father and brother.

What you can focus on here are the powerful experiences that highlight Billy's purpose as he struggles to overcome the stagnation, economic deprivation and prejudice in his community and how his experiences shape and alter the attitudes of those around him. Through Billy's passion for dance he drags his family into new experiences that shape their lives and alter existing assumptions and motivations. We see his father, a staunch unionist, break the picket lines for Billy, a complete change of heart as he is a father first and his son's passion changes his thinking and perspective on the world. They also have new physical experiences such as going to London which makes them see the world differently. Now we can look at some specific examples in the following sections.

Human Experiences through Dance and Music

Dance is a major theme within the film as not only is it a means of self-expression for Billy but it also functions as a means of liberation, opening up new experiences for Billy and those around him. The theme of dance was so important that the film was originally called *Dancer*. The theme is established early in the film through the song 'Cosmic Dancer' played as part of the soundtrack in the main titles. Like the young protagonist, the lyrics state

> I was dancing when I was twelve
> I was dancing when I was aaah
> I danced myself right out the womb
> Is it strange to dance so soon
> I danced myself right out the womb
>
> I was dancing when I was eight
> Is it strange to dance so late
> I danced myself into the tomb
> Is it strange to dance so soon
> I danced myself into the tomb

http://www.azlyrics.com/lyrics/trex/cosmicdancer.html

It is dance that allows Billy to make his journey into the world, to grow beyond the limitations of his family and community, to experience things and places like London that they have never had the experience of before. To be a professional dancer is Billy's dream and the message of the film is to definitely follow your dreams. His dream is met with opposition through society's gender expectations that dancing is only for girls. Billy dances throughout the film despite what his disapproving father says. This part of his experience gives him strength of character and builds his dream and motivation to succeed. When he experiences dance he is changed physically and emotionally.

The infectious physicality and energy of the dance sequences display a sense of freedom framed by a long shot. The long shots not only allow responders to engage with Billy's dancing but they also show how Billy relates with his environment; his world. Billy's world revolves around dance. Billy's gestures that express anger and frustration are also rhythmic and dance like. For example in the scene where Jacky Elliot finds out about the audition and bans him from dancing, Billy runs out of the house. There he begins to pull his face and stamp his feet but this turns into an expressive dance sequence.

Many of the songs on the soundtrack are performed by T. Rex who had many hits in the seventies. T. Rex is an English Glam Rock group led by the creative direction of guitarist / vocalist Marc Bolan. The band often performed with sequined costumes, heavy make-up teamed with a feather boa ad matching platform shoes. The band where still regarded to be popular within the youth culture. Glam Rock artists were not afraid to express themselves through their dress as well as their music. The soundtrack therefore transcends gendered stereotypes.

During the height of T-Rex's popularity in the seventies, it is assumed that the music belongs to Tony. Tony has some creative influence over his little brother. Billy brings as a tape that belongs to Tony for music to develop the audition piece to and he also likes to play Tony's records. This brings into play the concept that we can have shared experiences and develops the idea we can have further experiences from these. While the brothers gain different things from the music it has a shared and influential effect on both of them.

The Director, Stephen Daldry, says that the movie is more than the story of a boy who wants to dance, *Billy Elliot* "is a film that celebrates the human spirit[2]".

2   Allen, Jamie (2000) 'Billy Elliot' leaps into theatres, www.cnn.com/2000/SHOWBIZ/Movies/10/12/billy.elliot/

Human Experiences – Growing up

The film is primarily based around the story of how Billy grows up amidst the hardship of family turmoil and the adversity caused by the miners' strike in the greater community.

Daldry also says,

> "I don't think it's a film about dance...I think it is a film about going through your family and leaving your family and the bittersweet element of growing out and growing up and moving on."[3]

Billy grows up into the world of professional dance. In the letter Billy's mother wrote to him, she tells him to be true to yourself. Billy heeds this advice and remains true to his passion while growing up. It is these experiences that shape Billy as a man and they give him the strength of character to pursue a dream that others cannot see.

Billy is not the only character in the film that grows up through the experience of living in the town during a tough time. Michael is also seen growing up throughout the film and while his experiences are similar they have very different outcomes. He also had to face the barriers that Billy faced, those of the socio economic problems caused by the miners' strike and the community's ideological beliefs about what his appropriate behaviour for girls and boys.

Michael was brave enough to confide his sexuality with his best friend. Further evidence of Michael growing up is on Billy's big night where Michael is watching the performance with his partner.

---

3   Ibid

© Five Senses Education Pty Ltd

The character is wearing a flamboyant headdress as part of his costume. Like Billy, Michael was true to himself and the experiences he has are eventually positive and don't need to remain hidden because of the pre-conceived attitudes of others.

Adults can grow up too. Jacky Elliot also becomes a better person as he deals with his the death of his wife, forcing him to raise his two sons on his own. In accepting his son's passion for dance, he has also developed a closer relationship with him.

This can be seen in the scene of the medium close ups of Jacky and Billy joking around after they have received the good news of the letter. The framing focuses on how they have become closer as father and son. The natural lighting of this scene also creates a positive atmosphere suggesting that this is a new day for father and son. Thus the experiences that were negative such as his father's bullying machismo have dissipated into understanding.

Human Experiences – Gender

Gender is defined as the cultural construction of femininity or masculinity; the notion of the appropriate behaviour for either gender and how this is maintained ideologically. It includes everything a person does from the clothes they wear, the job that they have and of course recreational activities such as ballet. An individual may be male but have feminine attributes according to what their society regards to be female. The contrary is true where a female may also display male characteristics. Gender is distinct from sex, which is the biological difference between males and females. Gender therefore describes the ways in which masculinity and femininity serve ideologically to maintain a particular status quo in society. For example the prevailing belief of the society within *Billy Elliot* is that ballet is for girls and that boys should play football or participate in wrestling or boxing.

Gender is explored through the main plot of Billy's desire to become a dancer, where dance is the preserve of girls and homosexuals. Boys should be working out at the punching bag rather than performing pliés at the barre. The film argues that boys can also dance and that society should not be limited to stereotypical experiences.

The character of Michael also represents gender. Michael functions as the alternative to the heterosexual protagonist. Throughout the film, Michael displays feminine attributes that Billy accepts with an open heart. Michael seems to have a crush on his best friend who accepts him as he is but does not reciprocate those feelings. The film displays non-judgemental values of forgiveness and tolerance.

Questions for Human Experiences

- Discuss ONE human experience that shows how an attitude or anomaly in thinking by a character can be changed or altered. Be very specific in your response, using a quote(s) to support your ideas.

- Analyse ONE character other than Billy Elliot and discuss how that character contributes experience(s) to Billy's growth and development as a person and dancer.

- Describe the role and use of dance in two scenes from the film. How does the dance help represent ideas based on human experiences?

- How does the concept of gender play a role in engaging people in new experiences in the film?

- Describe in detail ONE aspect of growing up that highlights how one motivating factor can alter an existing idea and reflect on a personality through an experience.

- Comment on the shots used in TWO specific scenes from Billy Elliot, based on interactions within the family, and how they contribute to human experiences.

LANGUAGE

By now you should be familiar with the language devices that create meaning with film. Remember that for this Common Module you are to analyse how the notion of Human Experiences has been represented by the language of film. Although the dialogue is very important and should pay an important part in your analysis, film is also a visual medium. Therefore you need to be aware of visual language. Use the general film glossary at the beginning of this study guide. It is important to use this terminology in your responding and composing. Quotes from the film are included in the summaries and analysis section of this book.

Some of the main language features to consider are:

- Structure
- Production design
- Framing
- Editing and
- Mise-en-scène.

Structure

The structure and sequence of the film conforms to a regular narrative structure. The orientation is established early in the film. The historical and social context is developed in the scenes of The Main Titles and A Disgrace in The Gloves. The complication is of course Billy's struggle against the expectations of his family and community so that he can fulfil his dream to become a professional dancer. There are many heart-breaking moments that lead to the climax of the audition, interview and acceptance letter. The dance of defiance is a hinge even that changes the course of the narrative. The denouement is the excitement of adult Billy's first leap as a principal ballet dancer.

Production design

The location of the production design is central to the narrative. The mining town is an important aspect of the setting within the greater mise-en-scène. Many of the scenes are shot outside on location and not subject to the technological marvels of modern studios. Stephen Daldry set the fictional mining town of Everington in the real Easington where many of the locals still held strong feelings about the strike. The bleak industrial buildings and metallic structures provide a realistic backdrop to the action and visualise the toughness of the working class mining community. The setting of the scene A Ghost Story is the impressive Middlesbrough Transporter Bridge which dominates the backgound of Mrs Wilkinson and Billy, as they are contemplating the audition.

Framing

The framing is another film device that explores the relationship that the characters have with each other and their environment. Long shots combined with high camera angles are often used to portray the protagonist feeling overwhelmed by their situation. An example where this occurs was when Jacky and Billy Elliot step into the Royal Ballet School in London. The aerial long shot depicts the unfamiliarity of this new world. The marble interior of the building engulfs the figure suggesting that they have no control over this environment. If fact, they are now subject to the rules and value systems of the elite world of the Royal Ballet School. Long shots are also used to portray contrasting expressions of freedom where the long shots of Billy dancing are also juxtaposed with the shot sized used to frame Billy trapped within Everington. When Jacky Elliot accepts that his son is going to become a dancer, the developing relationship between father and son is portrayed using medium close ups. The medium close ups suggest a sense of intimacy that has evolved since Jacky has widened his gender based values.

Walls are also used as framing devices that symbolise the restrictions that are preventing Billy from fulfilling his dream. An example where this occurs is in the scene, the Chance to Dance. Once Billy is told that he can no longer dance he is shown in a dance sequence to be taking his frustrations out by dancing into the wall. The first wall that his dances into is the brick red wall of his own house. The framing of this wall at a high camera angle presents the wall as an ominous obstacle, one that the young protagonist cannot climb over.

Editing

The editor decides how long the shot will be and how the transitions between shots are made. Editing has an important function in creating the pace and rhythm of the film. Many of the dance sequences incorporate rhythmic editing when the transitions between shots are in time to the beats of the musical soundtrack. Fast paced editing will enhance the emotional intensity of the dance sequence. For example in the dance sequence after Billy misses out on the Newcastle audition due to Tony's incarceration. The argument between Tony and Mrs Wilkinson is edited rhythmically to the song 'Town Called Malice.' Not only do the lyrics of the song reinforce the animosity that Tony holds, the quick transitions of the rhythmic editing is also symbolic of Billy's confusion over his desire to dance and his family responsibilities.

Mise-en-scène

Mise-en-scène refers to the deliberate composition of a frame. It involves everything that is put in the frame such as lighting, costume, make-up, props and the physical movement of the figures. Lighting has a key role in creating atmosphere within a film. The dull overcast light of the scene where Billy visits his mother's grave with his grandmother adds to the sad nostalgic emotions. On the other hand the bright naturalistic lighting at the same setting when Billy revisits his mother's grave with his father creates a happy atmosphere between the now close father and son. *Low-key lighting* is used to enhance the feeling of suspense when Billy enters his first private ballet lesson with Mrs Wilkinson in the boxing club. This lighting emphasises Billy's shadow, as he hesitantly enters the club. *Backlighting* is also used in this scene around the figure of Mrs Wilkinson. She is in silhouette at the beginning of this scene. This also makes her look mysterious suggesting that Billy is unsure about what she expects of him.

The costumes and props reinforce the character types. The Elliot family wear what is expected of a middle class family from northern England that is faced with their present economic situation. The colour of their clothes is generally restricted to a dark palette based upon navy and the dark blue of denims. This is also symbolic of the futility caused by the miners' strike. Although Michael wears a similar costume to Billy, his costume is a reflection of his growth and development as he experiments with his sexuality. The dress that we see him try on is a bright green colour. This suggests that he does not have any negative feelings about what he is wearing; rather he sees it as fun.

When we first see Mr Wilkinson he is holding a glass filled with what we assume to be alcohol. This immediately signifies to the audience that he is associated with drink and it is later revealed by his daughter that he is an alcoholic. Mrs Wilkinson's cigarettes are similar in that she is not really focused on teaching her ballet lessons because she is too busy lighting them to pay attention to what her students are performing.

Remember to interpret these techniques in terms of human experience. Use them to support your ideas and develop a complexity of experiences that you can call on when developing your arguments. For example think about how any of these techniques enhance and reinforce the experience for the character(s) and what this says about human experiences.

Questions for Language Elements

- Discuss the impact of the basic narrative of the film. It follows the pattern of the heroes' journey as devised by Joseph Campbell and is a constant theme in human storytelling. Do you see Billy Elliot as a hero?
- Analyse how much film technique is used in one scene and the manner in which it is edited. What other techniques are used this scene? We need to remember that the scene you choose should say something about human experience. Do you think from your experience watching the film changed your attitudes to any of the film's ideas?
- Analyse the role and use of music in ONE scene from *Billy Elliot*. How does the music help represent ideas?
- Discuss the use of mise-en-scène in the film.

- Describe how production design contributes to Billy's experience(s) in the film. Use specific examples from the text to support your ideas.
- Comment on the shots used in TWO specific scenes from *Billy Elliot* and how they contribute to the idea of human experiences.

THE ESSAY

The essay consists of the basic form of an introduction, body paragraphs and conclusion. The esssay has been the subject of numerous texts and you should have the basic form well in hand. As teachers, the point we would emphasise would be to link the paragraphs both to each other and back to your argument (which should directly respond to the question). Of course, ensure your argument is logical and sustained.

Make sure you use specific examples and that your quotes are accurate. To ensure that you respond to the question, make sure you plan carefully and are sure what relevant point each paragraph is making. It is solid technique to actually 'tie up' each point by explicitly coming back to the question.

When composing an essay the basic conventions of the form are:

- State your argument, outline the points to be addressed and perhaps have a brief definition.

A solid structure for each paragraph is:
- Topic sentence (*the main idea and its link to the previous paragraph/ argument*)
- Explanation/ discussion of the point including links between texts if applicable.
- Detailed evidence (*Close textual reference – quotes, incidents and technique discussion.*)
- Tie up by restating the point's relevance to argument/ question

- Summary of points
- Final sentence that restates your argument

As well as this basic structure, you will need to focus on:

Audience – for the essay the audience must be considered formal unless specifically stated otherwise. Therefore, your language must reflect the audience. This gives you the opportunity to use the jargon and vocabulary that you have learnt in English. For the audience ensure your introduction is clear and has impact. Avoid slang or colloquial language including contractions (like 'doesn't', 'e.g.', 'etc.').

Purpose – the purpose of the essay is to answer the question given. The examiner evaluates how well you can make an argument and understand the module's issues and its text(s). An essay is solidly structured so its composer can analyse ideas. This is where you earn marks. It does not retell the story or state the obvious.

Communication – Take a few minutes to plan the essay. If you rush into your answer it is almost certain you will not make the most of the brief 40 minutes to show all you know about the question. More likely you will include irrelevant details that do not gain you marks but waste your precious time. Remember an essay is formal so **do not** do the following: story-tell, list and number points, misquote, use slang or colloquial language, be vague, use non-sentences or fail to address the question.

PLAN:

Don't even think about starting without one!

Introduce...

the texts you are using in the response

Argument: The human experience is affected by:

- Idea One
- Idea Two
- Idea Three

You need to let the marker know what texts you are discussing. You can start with a definition but it can come in the first paragraph of the body. You MUST state your argument in response to the question and the points you will cover as part of it. Wait until the end of the response to give it!

Idea One – Aspect of human experience as outlined in the textual material, e.g. physical impact.

Idea Two – Another aspect of human experience as outlined in the textual material, e.g. psychological impact.

- explain the idea
- where and how is it shown in the prescribed text?
- where and how is it shown in related text 1?

Idea Three – People's sense of experience is affected by context and environment

- explain the idea
- where and how shown in the prescribed text?
- where and how shown in related text 1?

You can use the things you have learned to organise the essay. For each one, you say where you saw this in your prescribed text and where in related text(s).

Two or three ideas are usually enough as you can explore them in detail.

- Summary of two key ideas
- Final sentence that restates your argument

Make sure your conclusion restates your argument. It does not have to be too long.

© Five Senses Education Pty Ltd

MODEL ESSAY OUTLINE

> **To what extent are human experiences significant in the set text?**
>
> **From your studies respond to this question using your set text and at ONE piece of other textual material**

This essay needs to be attacked in a manner that responds to the question and shows ALL your knowledge about the text. The question lends itself to a close study of Stephen Daldry's *Billy Elliot* as the text does show how the human experience is integral to life and how it shapes our other experiences and interaction with the world.

An introduction might be written:

> Human experiences are important in Daldry's film *Billy Elliot* and the two related texts Lawrence's film *Jindabyne* and Ed Sheeran's song *Castle on the Hill*. These texts show how human experiences are integral to human existence and bring more meaning to one's life. Life is about experiences that challenge us and define how we see the world. They shape our beliefs and attitudes and can be confronting at the same time. Without experiences our lives would be empty and meaningless.

Your essay should then follow the outlined plan and develop these ideas. This gives you the opportunity to link the texts and fully develop each of the ideas.

ANNOTATED RELATED MATERIAL: DIFFERENT STUDIES OF HUMAN EXPERIENCES

Jindabyne – Ray Lawrence

Jindabyne is an Australian film that captures a wide array of human experiences. It touches on the ideas mentioned in the introduction to this text in a number of detailed instances. We can begin by considering the following before beginning a detailed examination of the narrative.

The collective human experience:

- Aboriginality and the spiritual;
- The Fishermen and their code;
- The reaction of the townsfolk;
- Media response;
- Interaction with the natural world.

Individual Experience:

- An individual character's response to the body – choose one;
- The killer;
- Response to the revelations;
- Past experiences and how they impact on current experiences;
- Reaction to loss – emotional;
- Assumptions about life.

We can now look at the plot to help us understand each of these issues. *Jindabyne* begins with the sound of a radio being tuned and the Australian feel of the movie is immediate with the theme music for the ABC news. Lawrence emphasises the isolation by having the radio not tune in correctly for an unknown female character, forcing her to use the cassette player. With this unusual beginning we know that her experience is not going to be positive.

We then pan to the rocks slowly where Gregory, our killer, sits patiently in a truck with the engine running watching the road. We know he is prepared for this as he has binoculars. He sees an Aboriginal girl, Susan O'Connor, driving and she is the one fiddling with the radio. He chases her down and forces her to stop. He moves toward her as we see a long shot of how isolated they are. We see his face in her window looming above her and screaming about the electricity coming down from the mountains. This film is no murder mystery, as we know from the beginning that the murderer is Gregory the electrician. This is about the experiences of the other characters in the film and how they respond to current experiences.

The Kane family, Stewart, Claire and son Tom, is waking. Claire pretends to sleep, before waking suddenly and being affectionate with Tom. Stewart and Tom head out fishing. The scene doesn't feel quite right and there is some emotional tension between Stewart and Claire that is unspoken due to what they have experienced in the past. Claire had a complicated past when she was pregnant with Tom. When she finds she is pregnant again, she becomes emotional and slightly unstable.

As the film builds we see the complex pasts of the characters and their interactions in the confinement of the small town. The fishing trip is a break from this and extremely important in their lives.

We see some of the emotional instability in characters such as Caylin-Calandria, who with Tom, has some issues at school. Along with Caylin-Calandria, Claire and Jude also have issues but in a nicely framed shot of the three female characters, we see them conform as members of a close knit group. The sacrifice they make is similar to Gregory's but on a different scale. Note the connection here and how each one is to get back to order and societal norms. This is the collective experience for all the characters.

At the Kanes' home the tensions are obvious from their past experiences but they contain it for appearances' sake. Occasionally, the tension reaches breaking point and the experience strains the superficial approach. The tension builds at home and the fishing trip seems like a good opportunity to break the cycle.

When we see Gregory dump Susan O'Connor's body in the river, we know that the fishing and her death will interact.

The next morning, the fishermen head off for their one big trip of the year and the sign 'Gone fishing' is put in the garage window. We see Billy on the phone to Elissa and putting the sign the wrong way round in the window shows his immaturity. They have already said they are taking him away to make a man of him. The four men have a few beers on the way and talk as they travel through the landscape. They intend to give Billy the experience they think he needs as a 'man' — a cultural rite of passage.

The men arrive and the high-tension electricity wires punctuate the wilderness. They begin to hike toward the valley. It's a long walk in and the terrain is hilly and difficult. They stop on the way and again we see Billy's naivety when Stewart says 'Listen to that' meaning the silence but he can't, as he has his earphones in. It is part of the break in tension of the film that they commune with nature. This experiential break affects all the men. The episode represents a distinct human experience.

Stewart wanders down the river fishing and sees Susan's body caught in the rocks. Hesitantly, he wades out to it and turns it over saying 'Oh Jesus' repeatedly. He screams for the others to come as he drags the body to the bank. He is obviously upset, making the sign of the cross. Stewart tells Rocco to 'take her, for fuck's sake, take her' and their shock is obvious. They all stare at the body and Billy goes to run off but they stop him. The four men meet and decide to leave her in the water and tie her so she doesn't float away.

The presence of the body threatens to detract from the enjoyment of the fishing experience. The act of attempted isolation of the bad experience is expected to evoke only a mild response. They do not anticipate the stormy reaction it receives when they return to the community.

The men go on fishing, with Stewart getting the first big fish on an absolutely perfect day. The lure of the fish is strong, especially when they see the big one he has caught. They have a successful and enjoyable time, a positive experience. They get a photo of the catch and Billy holds up his fish in a typical hunter/gatherer pose. Capturing an experience this way is most enjoyable.

It is a photo that will come back to haunt them as things change back in the world. An unanticipated adverse reaction can be a horrific experience.

Stewart goes to check on the dead girl, rolling her over and getting debris off her face in a quite tender gesture. The next day they head back and report it. At the car Billy rings Elissa and says they found a body but 'caught the most amazing fish'. They are told by the police to wait and seem despondent their trip has been ruined. They organise their story as Stewart says they have 'to get their story straight'.

We cut to Gregory eating breakfast and he appears to be a normal, lonely man until he goes out to his shed where he has hidden Susan's car and this reminds us of the evil in him. Consider his experience and his motivations. How does he see his actions and the world?

The next day at the station the policeman tells the fishermen 'we don't step over bodies for our recreational pursuits' and 'the whole town's ashamed of you'. When they are told to 'piss off' from the station the press are waiting for them and Billy makes a comment. Carl is angry with the press but we can begin to see signs of distress within the whole group.

The experience they had so looked forward to has become a negative one and the tensions we saw before are exacerbated by the emotional and collective response to the murder. Claire soon becomes obsessed with the whole affair because of her own state. The newspaper the next day has the headline, 'Men fish over dead body' because Billy has talked. Billy is late to work and Stewart tells him they have to 'stick together on this'.

Susan's sister calls them 'animals' and raises the race question by asking if they would have left a white girl. The Aboriginal youths begin to attack and vandalise the property of the men in violent outbursts, including throwing a rock through Billy's van window and thus endangering his baby. They insult Carl at the caravan park and vandalise the garage.

The police aren't any help and the situation deteriorates. Jude tells the police they shouldn't be enforcing the 'political correctness' laws. The intervention of the sense of Aboriginality and race challenges the assumptions people have and how we see the world. The contrasting views are ingrained in the social structures and part of different collective experiences.

The Aboriginal people see the white people as 'interfering' and the group of fishermen begin to fight amongst themselves. Elissa says they shouldn't go to the bush at all as it's sacred. The group talk about the bush and Rocco punches Stewart for saying the Aborigines are superstitious. The experience of racial tension becomes ever-present and adds to the emotional responses to the experience.

We now head slowly to a resolution of the conflict brought about by the various experiences. Each is handled in a different manner by characters and you can explore one or two of the responses. To cycle back to the original murder, Claire is stalked by Gregory in his truck. He stops her but drives off after staring weirdly, an odd experience in itself.

Terry and Stewart talk and Stewart meets Rocco and Carl. He tells them Claire's left him 'again'. Rocco can't believe it and we cross cut to her looking out into the wilderness after he looks thoughtfully out the window. These different reactions to experiences mirror attitudes in life and reactions to emotional and intellectual conflict.

In conclusion, Lawrence takes us back to the healing power of nature in our human experiences when the Aboriginal people are having a ceremony. Gregory watches while Claire walks in. Again we see his truck as an omnipresent force in the film, almost an extension of him. An Aboriginal man tells Claire to 'piss off' from the ceremony after she says she has come to pay her 'respects' but he is told to leave her alone by an Auntie.

The smoke and tribal music symbolise the ceremonial nature of the setting and the camera pans around the scene and the bush. We see parts of the ceremony with chanting and clapping sticks. The camera moves in and out while other shots pan around the bush, giving us the full experience and Lawrence portrays this as a positive, healing experience.

Eventually Stewart, Tom, Carl, Jude and Rocco arrive to pay respects. Tom runs to his mother and Stewart goes over and says 'Sorry' but is rebuffed by the father who throws dirt on him and spits, refusing his apology. Then an Aboriginal girl tells a little about Susan's story and sings the last love song Susan wrote.

The camera pans around all the faces as they listen to the song and the ceremonial smoke wafts around. It seems to have some healing effect on everyone, as it is a meaningful experience which raises the idea of the spiritual experience in the text. The girl stops singing through emotion. 'Be gone' seems to symbolise in language the whole scenario for each character.

We see a long wide shot of the bush before fading back to Gregory waiting again in his car behind the rocks for another victim. It is quite a circular conclusion and it is an odd end when he crushes the fly. We don't quite know what to make of the whole experience and he seems to be the only character unchanged by the experiences in the film.

Poem: 'Inland' by John Kinsella

The poem captures the mood and ethos of the outback farming communities and deals with the human aspect more than some of the other poems in Kinsella's collection: *Peripheral Light*. This poem is one long restless thought that mimics memories and recollection while raising the current, topical issues that concern the poet. As usual with his poems Kinsella orientates the audience early with the word 'Inland' and then continues the poem without a full stop. The poem flows with the use of commas but Kinsella allows us to stop and think with the use of the colon, brackets and the hyphen. Look for these punctuation stops as you read as they emphasise a specific point or idea that resonates with the audience.

The first stanza gives us a foreshadowing of the events to follow with the warnings in the words 'storm', 'alert' and 'uncertain'. This ominous tone is reinforced by the word 'ghosts' and the implication of death which is constant in much of Kinsella's poetry. The next stanza deals with a more human element and we get the country feel with the bracketed gossip about McHenry's accident which shows the close knit community. Habits here are formed as part of survival and known to all as we see 'the old man plying the same track' and the families possibly heading to church on the Sunday morning.

The third stanza returns to the vagaries of nature. Kinsella repeats 'uncertain' with regard to the weather. Weather and the environment play a large role in farming communities and it is especially so at sowing and harvest. Despite the uncertainty and 'ashen' days which alter 'moods', the community returns to their habits and routines which shape their lives. The next stage returns to the road and the implication of a journey but a journey that is straight and in conflict with the cycles of the natural world. The path seems already marked and measured. It is 'straight and narrow', marked by a theodolite.

The final four lines of the poem are pure Kinsella, marking the transience of humanity on the landscape. We read

> 'it's a place of borrowed dreams
> where the marks of the spirit
> have been erased by dust –
> the restless topsoil'

The European farmers had 'borrowed dreams' for their own relationship with the land but this line also harks back to the indigenous Dreamtime when the land was created. The indigenous view that the land owns the people is also true for Kinsella. This sense of nobody owning the land is strong in his poetry. European impact on the land can be seen in the spirituality being removed by the dust—dust created by the poor farming techniques transferred from a different land. He finishes with the 'restless topsoil' as if the whole earth is moving in its own discontented journey, just as the people move.

The influence here of genuinely lost spirituality and connection with the land as we move directly on the 'high road' contrasts with the more flowing, 'restless' side of the natural world. This visual contrast is obvious but we can also discuss the contrast between habit and spirit. 'Inland' is a poem that uses the landscape to show the contrast between two views of the countryside.

DRAMA: Eugene O'Neil's *Desire Under the Elms*

O'Neill sets out to instruct how the house and elms should appear and the year is 1850. Note how he describes the 'enormous' elms as,

> 'exhausted women resting their sagging breasts and
> hands and hair on its roof, and when it rains their tears
> trickle down monotonously and rot on the shingles'

and how they dominate and 'rot'. It is important to read this both in terms of the play and in the context of American theatre. The description here shows O'Neill's genius at new design and original theatricality.

Part One: Scene One

The whole first page and a third are nearly all playwright notes that describe the farm, the house and the characters of Eben, Simeon and Peter. The first words of the play, 'God! Purty!' reflect the beauty of the land and how Eben perceives it. Eben is 'resentful and defensive' and feels 'trapped' on the farm.

His older half-brothers Simeon and Peter are 'more bounce and homelier in face, shrewder and more practical.' They all have worked hard on their father's farm over the years and have little feeling for their absent father. We learn that Simeon had a 'woman' who died and that Peter is excited by the prospect of 'gold in the West'. They all talk about how hard they've worked and hope that the father might 'die soon'. What we get from all this is that they are earthy and this is reflected in their bodies and clothes which are all dirt stained.

We also see here the difference between them as Eben sees gold in the pasture, not California, as they head in for a dinner of bacon in what seems a ritual they have performed many times before. Note that O'Neill calls for the use of the curtain at the end of the scene.

Scene Two

It is twilight and again we get detailed notes on the interior scene. Simeon tells Eben he should not wish their father dead and Eben replies he's not his son but, 'I'm Maw – every drop of blood!' He then blames the father, Ephraim Cabot, for killing his mother by working her to death but the others just say there was work to be done. O'Neill gets them to list the jobs and Eben comes back with 'vengeful passion' that, while they did nothing, he will see his mother gets 'rest and sleep in her grave!'

They then discuss Cabot's absence and how he just drove off in a buggy one day in a rush. Simeon says that when he went,

> 'He druv off in the buggy, all spick an' span, with the mare
> all breshed an' shiny, druv off clackin' his tongue an'
> wavin' his whip. I remember it quite well'

Eben mocks Simeon for not stopping him and the scene concludes with Eben leaving to see Minnie the town whore. We learn all the Cabot men have slept with her. Simeon and Peter say that Eben is just like 'Paw' and thinks of California. The final image is of Eben with his arms stretched to the sky talking about starts and sin, 'my sin's as purty as any one on 'em!', until he 'strides' to the village for Min.

Scene Three

It is 'pitch darkness' and Eben comes home with the news that Cabot has married a 'purty' thirty-five year old. He has heard this in the village and this effectively disinherits the boys. Simeon and Peter see California as their only option now. Eben tells the boys that they can have three hundred dollars each if they sign their share of the farm over to him. He can get the money as his mother told him,

> 'I know whar it's hid. I been waitin' – Maw told me. She knew whar it lay fur years, but she was waitin'....It's her'n – the money he hoarded from her farm an' hid from Maw. It's my money by rights now.'

They think about it and Eben tells them about his night with Min. He tells how he hates the new wife after the boys suggest he might sleep with her, just like Min, to get the old man back. Peter and Simeon say they'll do the deal and leave the farm. Both are bitter and vindictive about Cabot.

Scene Four

The setting is the same as Scene Two and the boys are discussing how they don't have to work now – it is all down to Eben who is jubilant as he thinks it will all be his. Peter and Simeon again reflect on how like his father he is, 'Like his Paw'. They also tell he isn't much of a milker but they soon talk about their leaving and how they'll miss some aspects of the farm.

Eben comes back in and says that the 'old mule an the bride' are coming. The two older boys begin to pack and sign Eben's papers as he gives them the money Cabot had hidden. They tell him they'll send him 'a lump o' gold for Christmas' and head into the yard feeling 'light' because of their newfound freedom.

Ephraim Cabot and Abbie Putnam then come in and O'Neill describes them in detail. Cabot is

> 'seventy-five, tall and gaunt, with great, wiry, concentrated power, but stoop shouldered by toil. His face is hard as if it were hewn from a boulder, yet there is a weakness in it'

but his face is weakened with petty pride. Abbie is

> 'thirty-five, buxom, full of vitality. Her round face is pretty but marred by its rather gross sensuality. There is strength and obstinacy in her jaw, a hard determination in her eyes, and about her whole personality.'

She also has a 'desperate quality'. Cabot shows Abbie the place and she says to him it's 'mine'. Then he sees the two boys not working. He introduces Abbie and she goes to look at 'her' house and they warn her Eben's inside.

Cabot tells them to get to work and they give him cheek, saying they are 'free' and heading to California. They 'whoop' it up and he says he'll have them chained up. They throw rocks at the house, smashing the window and head off singing. Abbie sticks her head out the window and says she likes the room but he is thinking of the stock and 'almost runs' to the barn.

Abbie then meets Eben in the kitchen and talks to him in 'seductive tones'. She says she doesn't want to be his 'Maw' but friends and he cusses her. She tells him of her troubled life and how Cabot gave her a chance to escape it. He calls her a 'harlot' and they argue over ownership of the farm. She has the upper hand in law and he leaves but the seeds of their growing attraction have been set.

Outside he and his father argue about life and work and he tells Eben 'Ye'll never be more'n half a man!' The scene ends with Abbie washing up and the faint notes of the song the boys were singing as they left.

Part Two: Scene One

Again O'Neill describes in detail the farmhouse setting. Two months have passed and it is a hot Sunday afternoon. Abbie in her best outfit is sitting on the porch and Eben comes out of the house also dressed in his best. They stalk each other, both attracted and repelled. As he walks away she 'gives a sneering, taunting chuckle' at him and they argue but the attraction is obvious. She says that nature will pull him to her but he says that she is married and he goes to leave her.

She accuses him of going to Min and she gets angry stating he'll never get the farm,

> 'Ye'll never live t' see the day when even a stinkin' weed on
> it 'll belong t' ye!'

He says he hates her and leaves as Cabot enters. She tells him Eben has been mocking him and twists the conversation to the inheritance of the farm. She tells him Eben lusts after her and as he angers she backs off in her accusations. Reassured, he says that she can have the farm if she bears the son she says she wants with him. He says that he'd 'do anythin' ye axed, I tell ye!' if she gave him a son and tells her to pray to God for it to happen.

Scene Two

It is about eight in the evening and here the bedrooms are highlighted, with Eben in one and Cabot with Abbie in the other. The two of them are talking about a son. They seem together, yet apart, as he tells her of his life on the farm and how God's hard. He both lost and gained on the way through, but the farm is his. He says he is pleased he found her, his 'Rose o' Sharon'. Abbie promises him that she will bear a son as he basically threatens her,

> 'Ye don't know nothin' – nor never will. If ye don't hev a son t' redeem ye...'

and he leaves to sleep in the barn with the cows 'whar it's restful'.

We then see Eben and Abbie restless and she leaves the room and goes to him. He 'submits' to her kisses then 'hurls' her away. Abbie says she'd make him 'happy' and she knows he wants her too much. She tells him to go down to the parlour and he is shocked as this is where his mother was 'laid out'. She leaves for the parlour and he wonders what's happening. The scene closes with a question to his dead mother, 'Maw! Whar are yew?' but we know that he wants her and will go to her.

Scene Three

The scene now shifts to the parlour which is described as a 'grim, repressed room like a tomb'. Abbie waits and Eben appears and he sits at her invitation. They talk about his Maw and how they hate Cabot. Abbie throws herself at him with 'wild passion' and he is caught up in the moment and thinks that it's his Maw wanting him to sleep with Abbie to get revenge on Cabot,

I see it! I sees why. It's her vengeance on him – so's she
kin rest quiet in her grave!

Abbie proclaims her love for him and he for her then they kiss 'in
a fierce, bruising kiss' to close the scene.

Scene Four

A more bold and confident Eben leaves the house and Abbie opens
the parlour window. She calls him over for a kiss and they talk a
bit before Eben says his Maw can now rest. They split as Cabot
comes out of the barn but are now obviously in love. Eben tells
Cabot that his Maw is now at rest and Cabot says he rests best
with the cows. Cabot is confused but the scene ends with him
criticising Eben as 'Soft-headed' and a 'born fool' but, being a
practical man, he heads for breakfast.

Part Three: Scene One

Time has passed to 'late spring the following year'. Eben is upstairs
in emotional and psychological conflict while a party happens
downstairs. Cabot has drunk too much and Abbie sits, pale and
thin, in a rocking chair. There is a fiddler and Abbie begins the
scene by asking for Eben and the guests 'titter' as most think the
baby is Eben's, not Cabot's, which is true enough. They laugh and
Cabot is angered by this and orders them to dance. The fiddler
'slyly' says they're waiting for Eben but Cabot mocks the boy and
then ensues a bawdy conversation about his fertility,

I got a lot in me – a hell of a lot – folks don't know on.
Fiddle 'er up, durn ye! Give 'em somethin' t' dance t!'

The fiddler plays and they dance. Cabot joins in frantically and 'whoop(s)' it up. He exhausts the fiddler and pours whiskey. In the upstairs room Eben is looking at the baby. Abbie goes upstairs and Cabot leaves for outside, 'fresh air', as she has told him not to 'tech' her. The guests gossip after he goes and we see Eben and Abbie upstairs and she professes her love for him,

> 'Don't git feelin' low. I love ye, Eben. Kiss me.'

Cabot says he's going to rest in the barn. The scene concludes with the fiddler playing in celebration of 'the old skunk gittin' fooled!'

Scene Two

Eben is outside half an hour later and Cabot is coming back from the barn. Cabot tells him to get a woman inside and he might get a farm. Eben replies that this farm's his and Cabot mocks him. He tells her Abbie has been promised the farm for her son and Eben is angered thinking Abbie has tricked him.

Eben goes to kill her but Cabot is too strong for him and Abbie comes out to stop him choking Eben. Cabot tells him he's weak and goes inside to celebrate. Abbie tries to be tender with Eben but he rejects her and calls her a liar.

> 'Ye're nothin' but a stinkin' passel o' lies. Ye've been lyin' t' me every word ye spoke, day an' night, since we fust – done it. Ye've kept sayin' ye loved me....'

She says she loves him and tells him that the promise was made before they fell in love. He says he'll go to California.

They argue and he 'torturedly' says he wished the baby had never been born. Abbie is distraught and she says she'd kill the baby to prove her love for him. He says he won't listen to her but she calls after him that she can 'prove' she loves him and she 'kin do one thin' God does'. Abbie is desperate at the end of the scene.

Scene Three

It is now just before dawn and Eben is in the kitchen ready to leave. Abbie is near the cradle with 'her face full of terror'. She sobs but Cabot stirs and she goes to the kitchen and flings her arms around Eben, kissing him 'wildly'. She says 'I killed him' and he thinks she means Cabot but is horrified when she tells him it's the baby.

Eben states it was his baby and she says she loved it but loves him more. He is angered,

> 'Don't ye tech me! Ye're pizzen! How could ye – t' murder
> a pore little critter – Ye must've swapped yer soul t' hell!

and tells her that he is getting the Sheriff and heads, 'panting and sobbing' to town. She calls out to him that she loves him.

Scene Four

It is after dawn and Abbie is in the kitchen. Cabot wakes in his room and is concerned that he has woken late. He checks the baby and is proud it is quiet and asleep. He goes down to Abbie in the kitchen and she tells him the baby is dead. He runs to check and comes back down and asks 'why?'

In a rage she tells him it was Eben's son and that she loves Eben, not him. He blinks back a tear and then gets 'stony' so he can carry on and says he is going to get the Sheriff. Abbie tells him that Eben's already gone so that Cabot tells her he'll 'git t' wuk.' He then tells her he'd never have told and now he's going to be 'lonesomer'n ever!' Eben comes back and Cabot tells him to get off the farm.

Eben asks for her forgiveness and tells her he loves her. He says he realised he loved her at the Sheriff's and they have a chance to run away but Abbie says she'll take her punishment. Eben says he will share it with her and plans to tell the Sheriff they planned it together. They think they can stand it together and then Cabot comes back.

He goes into a long tirade and tells them how he's let the stock go and will burn the house down. He too plans to go to California but finds that Eben has gotten to his money first. Cabot says that this is a sign from God to him to stay and that 'God's hard an' lonesome!' At this point the Sheriff comes and Eben says he was involved with the baby's murder.

Cabot says 'Take 'em both' and leaves to get his stock. The sun is coming up and as they are led away Eben says the farm's 'Purty' and Abbie agrees. The Sheriff finishes the play with the line, 'It's a jim-dandy farm, no denyin'. Wish I owned it!'

OTHER RELATED TEXTS

Fiction / Non-fiction / Drama

- *Wonder* – R G Palacio
- *First they Killed My Father* – Luong Ung
- *The Graveyard Book* – Neil Gaiman
- *Looking for Alaska* – John Green
- *Eleanor and Park* by Rainbow Rowell
- *The Fault in Our Stars* – John Green
- *We All Fall Down* – Robert Cormier
- *The Old Man and the Sea* – Ernest Hemingway
- *The Fire Eaters* – David Almond
- *Ender's Game* – Orson Scott Card
- *Hatchet* – Gary Paulsen
- *Inside Black Australia* – Kevin Gilbert
- *Sapiens: A Brief History of Humankind* – Yuval Noah Harari
- *Peeling the Onion* – Wendy Orr
- *Raw* – Scott Monk
- *Six Degrees of Separation* – John Guare
- *The Book Thief* – Markus Zusak
- *When Dogs Cry* – Markus Zusak
- *Holes* – Louis Sachar
- *The Outsiders* – S.E. Hinton
- *Roll of Thunder, Hear My Cry* – Mildred D. Taylor
- *A Small Free Kiss in the Dark* – Glenda Millard
- *Monster* – Walter Dean Myers
- *Lord of the Flies* – William Golding
- *Jandamarra* – Steve Hawke
- *A Separate Peace* – John Knowles
- *A Monster Calls* – Patrick Ness
- *The Pigman* – Paul Zindel
- *The Invention of Hugo Cabret* – Brian Selznik

- *Emerald City* – David Williamson
- *Silent Spring* – Rachel Carson

Films and Television

- *The Human Experience* – Charles Kinnane
- *My Brilliant Career* – Gillian Armstrong
- *Broadchurch* – James Strong & Euros Lyn
- *Twinsters* – Samantha Futerman and Ryan Miyamoto
- *Be My Brother* – Genevieve Clay - Smith
- *What's Eating Gilbert Grape* – Lasse Hallstrom
- *Pleasantville* – Gary Ross
- *Eternal Sunshine of the Spotless Mind* – Michel Gondry
- *Taxi Driver* – Martin Scorsese
- *Tootsie* – Sydney Pollack
- *Back in Time for Dinner* – Kim Maddever
- *The Godfather* – Francis Ford Coppola
- *Friends* – David Crane and Marta Kaufmann
- *Dawson's Creek* – Kevin Williamson
- *Orange is the New Black* – Jenji Kohan
- *Boy Meets World* – Michael Jacobs and April Kelly

Website – quote on literature and the human experience

http://view2.fdu.edu/academics/university-college/school-of-humanities/
english-language-and-literature-program/

At its most fundamental level literature explores what it means to be a human being in this world and tries to describe what our human experience is like. As such, literature pushes us to confront the large human questions that have plagued humankind for centuries: issues of fate and free will, issues relating to our role in the universe, our relationship to God, and our relationships with others. Studying literature not only helps us to understand the complexity of these questions intellectually, but because of its very nature, it allows us to experience these tensions vicariously. Literature does not just tell us about human experience; it recreates it in a way we can feel and visualise. In other words, it calls for a total response from us—it stretches us beyond who we are.

First, literature can enhance our ability to relate to people. Because literature focuses on human relationships and self perception, it can broaden our own experience—to help us understand different kinds of people, different cultures, different problems—and, consequently, help us better understand our own relationships with others.

The study of literature also helps to foster an appreciation for beauty, symmetry, and order. This means more than the intuitive response of liking or disliking something we see or read or hear; it means a carefully thought-through response that will enhance appreciation—not destroy it.

Perhaps the most important skills that the study of literature teaches are analytic and synthetic skills. In learning to read carefully and analytically, we learn to ask hard questions both of the work and of ourselves. And as we seek to discover the relationships between the ideas and images we uncover in a work, our ultimate goal is to see the whole—to see how the parts work together to make the piece what it is. In grappling with the complex and difficult ideas contained in literature, we learn to accept the multiple dimensions and ambiguity that are so often present in life.

Finally, the study of literature will also help develop our writing abilities as we come to value the written word and understand its power to communicate.

Beyond all of these skills, however, it is not what literature can do for us as individuals as much as what it can do to us. Literature speaks to the whole person. Listen to it, says C. S. Lewis, and you will be changed.

Poetry

- 'Warren Pryor' – Alden Nowlan
- 'The Gardener' – Louis MacNeice
- 'The Improvers' – Colin Thiele

Songs

- *Be My Escape* – Relient K
- *Mandolin Wind* – Rod Stewart
- *Roxanne* – The Police
- *Wake Me Up When September Ends* – Green Day
- *Under Pressure* – Queen & David Bowie
- *Candle in the Wind* – Elton John
- *Empire State of Mind* – Alicia Keys
- *Gold Digger* – Kanye West
- *We Are Young* – Fun.
- *Centrefold* – J. Geils Band
- *It's Time* – Imagine Dragons
- *We Cry* – The Script
- *If I Were a Boy* – Beyoncé
- *Shake it Out* – Florence + the Machine
- *C'mon* – Panic! At the Disco & Fun.
- *I Don't Love You* – My Chemical Romance
- *Sing* – My Chemical Romance
- *1985* – Bowling for Soup
- *What About Me* – Shannon Noll
- *Sinner* – Jeremy Loops
- *7 Years* – Lucas Graham

- *Bitter Sweet Symphony* – The Verve
- *Ghost!* – Kid Kudi
- *Good Riddance (Time of Your Life)* – Green Day
- *Expectations* – Belle and Sebastian
- *After Hours* – We Are Scientists
- *Write About Love* – Belle and Sebastian
- *Trust Your Stomach* – Marching Band
- *Heaven Knows I'm Miserable Now* – The Smiths